Essential
Melbourne

by
MAUREEN ERSKINE

Maureen Erskine has travelled extensively around the world, earning her living as a travel writer and journalist. She was born in Sydney, but has lived in Melbourne for over 20 years.

GW00703334

AA

Produced by the Publishing Division of
The Automobile Association

Written by Maureen Erskine
Peace and Quiet section by Paul
Sterry
Consultant: Frank Dawes

Edited, designed and produced by
the Publishing Division of The
Automobile Association. Maps ©
The Automobile Association 1991

Distributed in the United Kingdom
by the Publishing Division of The
Automobile Association, Fanum
House, Basingstoke, Hampshire,
RG21 2EA.

A CIP catalogue record for this book
is available from the British Library.

ISBN 0 7495 0095 6

Published by The Automobile
Association

Typesetting: Tradespools Ltd, Frome,
Somerset

Colour separation: BTB Colour
Reproduction, Whitchurch,
Hampshire

Printed in Italy by Printers S.R.L.,
Trento

Front cover picture: Melbourne

This book employs a simple rating system to help choose which places to visit:

 do not miss

 see if you can

 worth seeing if you have time

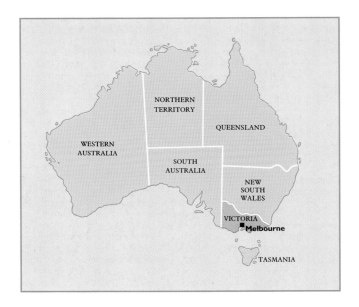

INTRODUCTION

Melbourne is about as far Down Under as you can go. It is the southernmost capital city on the vast mainland of Australia. Only the island state of Tasmania is further south, nearer the 'end of the earth'. Yet Melbourne, so far away from just about anywhere, is one of the great Victorian cities of the world. It abounds in the architecture of the last century—the grand and elegant, the flamboyant and frivolous, the picturesque terrace houses decorated with ornamental cast-iron lace-work. The buildings have aged well. Their mature façades sit comfortably amid the younger, slimmer and taller glass structures, which now mark the skyline of the city.
Melbourne is a city of great beauty. One-quarter of it is made up of magnificent parks and gardens. Its wide streets are lined with avenues of wonderful, century-old trees, which flood the city with gold in autumn.
It is a most sophisticated city, recognised as the cultural, commercial and culinary capital of Australia. It has countless art galleries, museums,

theatres and crafts. The city is also mad on sports, and has declared a public holiday on the day a horse race, the Melbourne Cup, is run! This is the country's most cosmopolitan city, settled by people from some 100 nations, and there are restaurants and cafés with cuisines from these countries to suit all tastes and budgets.

Melbourne is the capital of Victoria, the smallest state on the mainland; but its small size is a big advantage: its attractions are all very accessible. Most of Victoria can be reached in half a day's drive. You can leave 20th-century Melbourne and, within a few hours, walk through country which is part of one of the oldest land masses on earth, scarcely disturbed by humans. Victoria has an incredible variety of landscapes. Gentle undulating countryside, spectacular rugged coastline, miles of sandy beaches, vineyards, alps and rainforests. It has a great number of historic towns, with some architectural gems of buildings carefully restored from the gold rush days of the mid 1800s. You can see the unique and often shy Australian flora and fauna at close quarters: the koala, kangaroo, wombat, platypus, emu, lyrebird and fairy penguins. Victoria is the garden state of Australia, with wildflowers covering the countryside and beautiful private gardens to view.

In recent years, Victoria has become known through films and television series. Melbourne is the home of the television soap opera *Neighbours*, which has an estimated viewing audience of more than 20 million around the world. (Yes, Ramsey Street, where the series is set, does exist—in Melbourne—but this is not its true name!)

Melbourne has plenty to offer, even off-screen. You can cruise in old-fashioned style on a paddle steamer along the Murray River. You can picnic at Hanging Rock—although hopefully not with the same fatal and mysterious ending as in the film of that name! You can wander through the country where famous bushranger and folk hero Ned Kelly roamed and robbed. You can see the countryside around the exclusive school Timbertop, which the Prince of Wales attended.

Despite all these attractions, and more,

INTRODUCTION

Melbourne is often little more than a murmur in the ears of the tourists of the world. But when people do come here, they invariably fall for its charms.

Some of the city's attractions are not immediately obvious. Melbourne is made for walking—and that is how you discover so much. Look up to the roofline of the old buildings and you will see the most extraordinary decorations, from urns to faces. Follow the cobbled and flag-stoned laneways amid the wide boulevards, and discover markets, as well as department stores, old arcades and new shopping complexes. You can be in the centre of the bush, rowing along the Yarra River, simply by turning off a busy highway, less than 10 minutes' drive from the heart of the city.

Melbourne may be at the end of the world, but it has a world of things to see and do.

The Yarra River is a focal point and gathering place for Melburnians

BACKGROUND

Melbourne sits within the curve of Port Phillip
Bay, a large coastal inlet, 37 miles (60km) from
Bass Strait, the nearest open sea. The heart of
Melbourne is situated on the Yarra River, which
winds its way down from the Dandenong
Ranges, an hour's drive away. The Yarra
gracefully divides Melbourne in two: the main
central business district on one side, parklands
on the other. The Yarra's murky colour has led to
its reputation as the river which flows upside-
down; no amount of cleaning will make this silt-
carrying river crystal clear. However, fish still
survive and are caught in it, despite its colour.
The site for Melbourne was chosen in 1835 by
pioneer John Batman. His statement, or perhaps
understatement, has been well-quoted: 'This will
be the place for a village'. Australian-born
Batman had acquired some pastoral land in
Tasmania (then called Van Diemen's Land). He
heard about rich grazing lands on the mainland
from sealers and whalers who often called there.
Batman wanted to extend his land, and he and
others of similar ambition formed a group called
the Port Phillip Association. On their behalf
Batman sailed across Bass Strait and rowed up
the Yarra. He liked what he saw, and negotiated
to 'buy' the land from the local Aborigines. He
received 500,000 acres (200,000 hectares) 'more
or less' in exchange for '20 pairs of blankets, 30
tomahawks, 100 knives, 50 pairs of scissors, 30
looking glasses, 200 handkerchiefs, 100 pounds
of flour and six shirts' plus a promise of a yearly
rental of similar items. He signed a treaty with
eight tribal chiefs. There was one problem: the
Government declared the deed invalid. But it
was too late. Batman and others from Tasmania
had already settled on the land with their sheep
and cattle, and the Government was forced to
recognise the treaty. The 'squatters' stayed, and
the city of Melbourne was born. The original
deed is kept in the archives of the La Trobe
Library (see page 32).
The new colony was slow to progress. Then gold
was discovered in Victoria around Ballarat in
1851 and Melbourne, named after the British
Prime Minister, was re-born. The goldfields
proved to be among the richest the world had

BACKGROUND

Gold made Melbourne's fortune. You can still try your luck at Sovereign Hill

ever seen. People flocked to the area from all over the world to make their fortunes. The population of Melbourne multiplied rapidly. In the same year as the discovery of gold, the colony was separated from New South Wales and became the state of Victoria, named after Queen Victoria. The gold rush was over in the 1860s—but you can still find gold around the old goldfields with a modern metal detector.

Gold made Melbourne. It was a fabulously wealthy city. Foundation stones were laid for the city's grandest buildings: Parliament House, the Public Library, the University of Melbourne. These were the boom years for 'Marvellous Melbourne'; but a decade later came the economic slump. But the foundations were already established for Melbourne to be the great industrial and manufacturing city it is today. In 1901 the colonies of Australia became a federation and the Commonwealth of Australia was formed. Melbourne was the venue for the Federal Parliament, until Canberra was established in 1927.

Present-day Melbourne is one of the largest cities, in area, in the world. The Greater

Melbourne area covers 2,359 square miles (6,110sqkm), compared with Greater London's 602 square miles (1,560sqkm) or New York's 1,525 square miles (3,950sqkm). As in so many other cities of the world, the heart of Melbourne is being torn apart. In the last year of the 1980s whole blocks were being pulled down. Fortunately, this was not the complete destruction of the old. Some of the aged buildings have survived, between towering new blocks of glass; or their façades remain, while the new have been built within or behind them. Melburnians did not always love the ornamental cast-iron lace, as it is called, on terrace houses; they pulled it off in the 1950s, but had a change of heart in more recent times and started restoring it to its former beauty. Melbourne has retained its Victorian face but with many facelifts. Melbourne's population is over three million. Originally the settlers were British, but after World War II people flocked here from Europe, and in recent years more Asians, including Vietnamese, have come. Melbourne has retained many of its British features, such as gentlemen's clubs and 'public' schools which are, in fact, private schools. It has a conservative front and reputation—and yet there is a liveliness underneath, and its nightlife is punctuated with every type of music sound. Melbourne is often compared with Sydney, and there is a long-established rivalry between them. Sydney is described as more brash, more American, Melbourne more European. Melburnians concede that Sydney is a great place for a holiday, but they would not like to live there. Sydneysiders rarely express any desire to come to Melbourne—except perhaps for the Melbourne Cup! There are plenty of jokes about Melbourne's weather—its changeability and its tendency to rain. The fact is that Sydney's rainfall is much higher, but it is true that Melbourne's weather can be overcast and grey; it can drizzle or storm; can suddenly switch from hot to cold. But Melbourne has beautiful changes of seasons: the autumn, in March and April, can be especially lovely. And the brilliant sunsets more than make up for the occasional downpour. This is a city with many obvious and hidden delights: most visitors succumb to its charm.

AREAS OF THE CITY

The centre of Melbourne is very compact, and it is easy to find your way around. It is set out in a simple rectangular grid with criss-crossing, parallel streets.

The person responsible for its planning was Robert Hoddle, City Surveyor of the mid-1850s. He designed the wide streets which have enabled Melbourne to cope with its great volume of traffic today.

The boundaries of the city centre are from Flinders to La Trobe to the north and from Spencer to Spring Streets to the east. Between Flinders, which is closest to the river, and La Trobe, are Collins, Bourke and Lonsdale Streets. Between these are narrower streets, originally used for servicing purposes, each, except Flinders Lane, with the prefix 'Little': Little Collins, Little Bourke and Little Lonsdale Streets. Between Spencer and Spring Streets are King, William, Queen, Elizabeth (easy to remember in that royal sequence), Russell and Exhibition Streets. Melbourne's famous trams run along some of these streets (see page 39), travelling to the suburbs.

These streets are the heartbeat of Melbourne, having most of the main shops, hotels, offices and banks, as well as historic buildings and museums, with several parks near by.

The best way to feel the pulse of the city, to capture its flavour and atmosphere, is to walk around these streets: along the main thoroughfares or lanes, many of them filled with little shops or cafés, and through shopping complexes or arcades. And if you become tired, hop on a tram for a stop or two.

You can shop at Cartier or at the Queen Victoria Market; buy a Christian Dior shirt or a souvenir boomerang; have a sandwich in a snack bar or dress in your best and have luncheon at Fanny's, one of Melbourne's internationally acclaimed restaurants. The choice is yours to suit your taste—and your pocket.

Bourke Street

Parliament House lies across the top of Bourke Street, the busiest street in Melbourne, and dominates the medley of shops and eating

Wide streets in a grid setting are a feature of the lively city centre

places—which include The Society (no 23), one of Melbourne's oldest restaurants.

Crossing Bourke Street is Exhibition Street, notorious for its brothels in the 1870s, when this area was made up of slums, sly grog shops and cheap eating houses.

Between Swanston and Elizabeth Streets, Bourke Street is a pedestrian mall. But look out for the trams. They slide through the area at a snail's pace, but if you stray on the lines when they are moving, you will hear a loud clanging of bells to warn you to move out of the way. There are seats to sit amid trees and potted plants, but usually the Mall is a hive of activity, specially for the couple of hours after midday, when office workers flock to the Mall during their luncheon breaks.

Further down Bourke Street, between King and Spencer, amid rather mundane buildings, there is a gem of a little bluestone church: St Augustine's Roman Catholic Church, which sits within its own grounds. This solid structure was opened in 1888, and has an intricate timber ceiling, supported by rows of slender pillars.

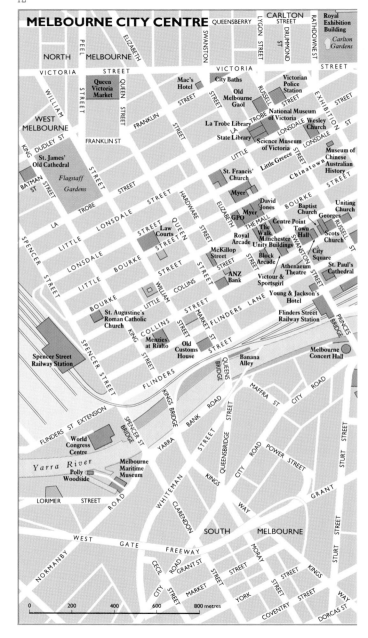

MELBOURNE CITY CENTRE

QUEENSBERRY
CARLTON STREET
LYGON STREET
DRUMMOND
RATHDOWNE ST
Royal Exhibition Building
Carlton Gardens

PEEL
ELIZABETH
SWANSTON

NORTH MELBOURNE

VICTORIA STREET
VICTORIA STREET

WILLIAM ST
WEST MELBOURNE

QUEEN STREET
Queen Victoria Market
QUEEN STREET
FRANKLIN STREET

Mac's Hotel
City Baths
Old Melbourne Gaol
Victorian Police Station
RUSSELL STREET
National Museum of Victoria
EXHIBITION ST
Wesley Church

FRANKLIN ST
La Trobe Library
LA TROBE STREET
State Library
Science Museum of Victoria
LONSDALE STREET
Little Greece
Chinatown
Museum of Chinese Australian History

KING STREET
DUDLEY ST
BATMAN ST
St. James' Old Cathedral

Flagstaff Gardens

LA TROBE STREET
HARDWARE STREET
St. Francis' Church
Myer
ELIZABETH STREET
BOURKE STREET

LONSDALE STREET

SPENCER STREET

LA TROBE

LITTLE LONSDALE

LONSDALE STREET
Law Courts
QUEEN STREET
David Jones
Myer
GPO
THE MALL
Royal Arcade
Manchester Unity Buildings
Centre Point
The Walk
Town Hall
SWANSTON STREET
Baptist Church
Georges
Scots Church
Uniting Church
RUSSELL ST

LITTLE BOURKE STREET
McKillop Street
Block Arcade
City Square
St. Paul's Cathedral

ANZ Bank
Athenaeum Theatre
Victour & Sportsgirl

BOURKE STREET
WILLIAM STREET
LITTLE COLLINS STREET
Young & Jackson's Hotel
PRINCES BRIDGE

St. Augustine's Roman Catholic Church
COLLINS STREET
MARKET STREET
FLINDERS LANE
Flinders Street Railway Station

Menzies at Rialto
KING STREET
Old Customs House
FLINDERS STREET
Banana Alley
Melbourne Concert Hall

Spencer Street Railway Station

SPENCER STREET

FLINDERS STREET

KINGS BRIDGE

FLINDERS ST EXTENSION
SPENCER ST BRIDGE
World Congress Centre

MAFFRA ST
CITY ROAD

BANK STREET
YARRA STREET
QUEENSBRIDGE STREET
CITY ROAD
POWER STREET

STURT STREET

Yarra River
Polly Woodside
Melbourne Maritime Museum

WHITEMAN STREET
KINGS WAY

LORIMER STREET
CLARENDON STREET

GRANT STREET

NORMANBY ROAD
WEST GATE FREEWAY
SOUTH MELBOURNE
MORAY STREET
STURT STREET

CECIL STREET
GRANT ST
CITY ROAD
MARKET STREET
STREET
KINGS WAY
COVENTRY STREET

| 0 | 200 | 400 | 600 | 800 metres |

YORK STREET
DORCAS ST

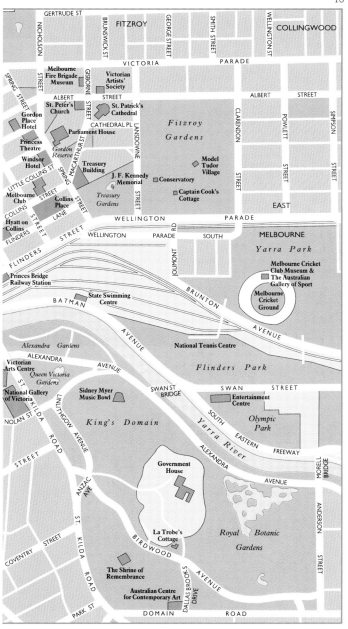

Collins Street

Collins Street is the best city address for offices
and shops. The top end has been called the
'Paris' end because of its lovely old buildings
and trees. Originally this was a fashionable
residential area for doctors, lawyers and
merchants, but over the years most of these
residences have been demolished and replaced
by modern glass edifices. No 1 is one of the few
former town houses still remaining.

Fortunately, in the late 1980s, the steady
demolition of the city's heritage was slowed
down, and some buildings of the past have been
reserved, restored and renovated.

One of the grandest buildings still standing is the
Melbourne Club (36–50), foremost gentlemen's
club in Australia, with a most delightful
courtyard, enclosed by a high wall. The Club
stands opposite the spectacularly modern

*Flinders Street
Railway Station is
an impressive
landmark*

Collins Place complex, which has giant twin
towers linked by a huge airy plaza, known as the
Great Space. This houses boutiques and eating
places and glass-walled lifts. One tower contains
offices; the other includes the Regent Hotel.
The Victorian Tourism Commission (Victour), at
230 Collins Street, is the official Government
information centre, where you obtain all you
want to know about Melbourne and Victoria
(open: Monday to Friday 09.00–17.00 hrs;
Saturdays 09.00–12.00 hrs).

Flinders Street

Flinders Street runs at right angles to Swanston
Street, alongside part of the river. You cannot
miss seeing Flinders Street Railway Station, the
multi-coloured brick building with its
clocktower and copper domed roof, situated
near the Yarra River and Princes Bridge. This is
the starting point for suburban trains, famous for
its face of clocks, which give the times of
departing trains; 'under the clocks' is a well-
established meeting place. The station was built
in 1854 on the site of a former fish market, to the
design of two railway employees.

Little Bourke Street

Walk along Little Bourke Street and you could
be in a back street of Hong Kong. This is
Melbourne's Chinatown, marked officially by
Oriental archways between Exhibition and
Swanston Streets, but some of the Chinese shops
and cafés spill over into nearby streets. The
Chinese first came to Victoria in large numbers
during the gold rush days of the mid 1850s, and
stayed in the cheap lodgings of Little Bourke
Street on their way to the goldfields. By the end
of the century, provision stores, Chinese
herbalists and cabinet makers abounded. Many
of the 19th-century Victorian buildings were
commissioned by Chinese businessmen and
designed by notable architects of the day; some
still stand. Small stores selling Chinese goods
and food now sit between more modernised
restaurants, which predominate in the street
today. There are more than 60 Chinese cafés,
ranging from the budget to the best. There are
also up-to-date establishments catering for the

Chinese: a travel agency, hairdressers, cake shop; and even the car park has Chinese characters as well as English on its notice board.

Lonsdale Street
Next to and running parallel to Little Bourke Street is Lonsdale Street. Here is an example of the close blending of two ethnic groups side by side. Between Russell and Swanston Streets, Lonsdale Street is Little Greece. Shops are packed with recordings, newspapers, children's clothes, cakes—all identifiably Greek. There are many Greek cafés, full of Greeks—but with the usual Greek hospitality, all are made welcome.
Lonsdale Street's attractions include St Francis' Church (see page 28) and the Law Courts (see page 25).

Spring Street
Spring Street, which runs along the top end of the two main streets Collins and Bourke, is only a comparatively short street, but it is full of some of the most flamboyant buildings in the city, including Parliament House (see page 25), the Treasury Building (page 27), the Windsor Hotel (page 82) and the Princess Theatre (page 89.)

Swanston Street
Swanston Street stretches a long way past the centre of the city to Carlton. It is very busy and bustling from Princes Bridge, as it is the main street for trams going southbound across the Yarra. St Paul's Cathedral is on the corner of Swanston Street and Flinders Street (see page 28), and next to it is the City Square. This has had a very chequered career since it was officially opened by Queen Elizabeth in 1980. A modern sculpture, dubbed the Yellow Peril, has come and gone (down to the Yarra Bank near the World Trade Centre). Plans for open-air cafés overlooking the square never really got off the ground. It should be a small oasis set between St Paul's and the Town Hall, but it has been not much more than a mini asphalt area with a few trees and noisy waterfalls, used for protest gatherings and rather cheap promotions. It is now being redeveloped again.

A forest of skyscrapers stretches above the greenery on the Yarra's banks

Yarra River

The river passes the city's front door, as it were, and from Princes Bridge is especially pretty on the parkland side. Alexandra Avenue is a beautiful tree-lined street, which runs alongside the river from the city to the suburb of South Yarra. The Yarra is not a busy river: occasionally you will see rowing eights practising, or tourist boats (cruises leave from Princes Bridge Wharf); and along its banks people walk or cycle (the south bank has a cycle track) and have picnics. To see the Yarra in a natural bush setting, go to **Studley Park Boathouse**, Boathouse Road, Kew (tel: 861 8707), only four miles (7km) from the city. It is one of the 'hidden' places of Melbourne, established in 1863, and here you can hire rowing boats or kayaks (open: daily, 09.30–18.00 hrs).

A similar style of place, but more commercialised, is **Fairfield Park Boat Shed**, Fairfield Park Drive, Fairfield (tel: 486 1501). To reach this spot, you come directly from a main highway, which makes it all the more surprising. The boathouse here is more grand and has been restored. There is a restaurant, and boats are for hire (open: 07.30–17.30 hrs).

AREAS OF THE CITY

The Suburbs

Melbourne has a wonderful mix of suburbs. People can choose to live by the bay, the river, the inner city or in natural bush areas. South Yarra and Toorak (see below) are the top suburbs to see; Toorak Road, which connects the two shopping areas, is full of interesting shops and restaurants. It's worth making the easy journey out from the city centre to explore these distinctive areas.

Carlton, nearly two miles (3km) north of the city, is Melbourne's Little Italy. Many Italians settled there in the 1950s and opened cafés and shops, and, though some have now moved to other suburbs, the atmosphere still remains. The suburb is full of students too, being close to the University of Melbourne (see page 27).

East Melbourne, is mainly residential, and has some of the prettiest streets in the city, with beautifully restored terrace houses featuring ornamental lace-work. The city centre is within walking distance, through Fitzroy and Treasury Gardens (see page 36).

Parkville, nearly two miles (3km) north of the city, is a suburb which lives up to its name. Its main street, Royal Parade, is one of the most magnificent boulevards in Melbourne, lined with elms planted more than 100 years ago. Parkville was once heavily forested and land

Victorian 'lace-work' graces Melbourne's restored terrace houses, now in fashion once again

was not sold for housing until 1867. It is still a very uncommercialised area, and is the setting for Melbourne's biggest park, Royal Park (see page 39). The houses are among the most beautiful and varied of the Victorian era, many boasting carved adornments of wreaths of fruit, shells, faces and urns.

St Kilda, nearly four miles (6km) south of the city, attracted visitors, in the early days of Melbourne, who came to enjoy the cool sea breezes off Port Phillip Bay. In the boom years of the late 1880s, the wealthy built large homes; a wooden pier, which still stands, was erected in 1857; and this became a popular place to live, away from Melbourne's dusty heat, and crowds. Over the years the character of the place changed. With the advent of rail and motor vehicles it became fashionable for the rich to go further afield. They chose Toorak to build their mansions, and made Queenscliff into a sophisticated seaside holiday resort. St Kilda went into decline. Many of the mansions were turned into apartments; some were pulled down. Fitzroy Street became a notorious strip for prostitution and drugs. In recent years, however, some of the large old houses have been re-discovered and renovated, and artists and writers have moved in.

St Kilda is now a place for cheap hotels and cheap eats, for art galleries and 'adult movie' shops. Grand old hotels have been turned into venues for music groups; one of the best known is the Victoria, built in 1859.

From St Kilda you can see the grand sweep of the bay, which curves all the way to Station Pier at Port Melbourne. This was once busy with the comings and goings of passenger liners on their way to and from Europe. Now the ships that come into the port are mainly cargo ships, with only the occasional cruise ship calling.

There are beaches from St Kilda to Port Melbourne, belonging to the suburbs of **Middle Park** and **Albert Park**. They have fine sand with grassy dunes and palm trees. Notices warn inexperienced swimmers that there can be a tricky undertow, but there is more lying on the beach than swimming. The beach opposite Kerferd Road is a topless beach and is a very popular place.

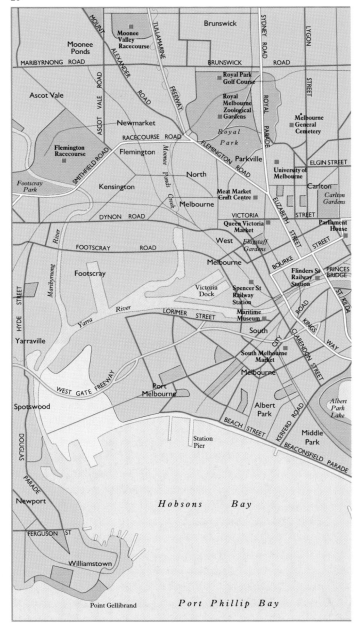

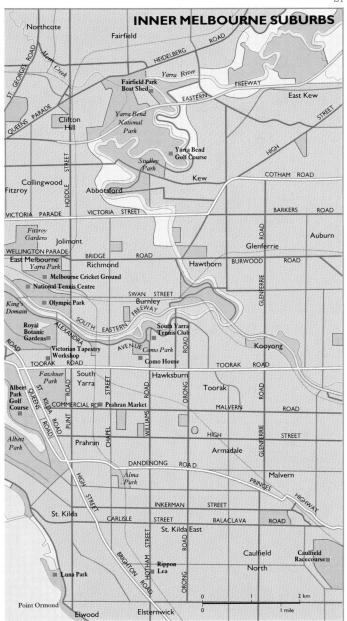

INNER MELBOURNE SUBURBS

Northcote
Fairfield
HEIDELBERG ROAD
Yarra River
FREEWAY
St GEORGES ROAD
Merri Creek
QUEENS PARADE
Clifton Hill
Fairfield Park Boat Shed
EASTERN
East Kew
HIGH STREET
Yarra Bend National Park
Yarra Bend Golf Course
Studley Park
Collingwood
COTHAM ROAD
HODDLE STREET
Fitzroy
Abbotsford
Kew
VICTORIA PARADE
VICTORIA STREET
BARKERS ROAD
Fitzroy Gardens
Jolimont
WELLINGTON PARADE
East Melbourne
Yarra Park
BRIDGE ROAD
Richmond
Hawthorn
BURWOOD ROAD
Glenferrie
Auburn
ROAD
GLENFERRIE
Melbourne Cricket Ground
National Tennis Centre
King's Domain
Olympic Park
SWAN STREET
Burnley
SOUTH EASTERN FREEWAY
ALEXANDRA
Royal Botanic Gardens
Victorian Tapestry Workshop
South Yarra Tennis Club
Como Park
Como House
AVENUE
ROAD
Kooyong
TOORAK ROAD
TOORAK ROAD
Faulkner Park
South Yarra
Hawksburn
STREET
ORONG ROAD
Toorak
Albert Park Golf Course
ST KILDA ROAD
QUEENS ROAD
COMMERCIAL RD
Prahran Market
PUNT ROAD
MALVERN ROAD
Albert Park
CHAPEL STREET
WILLIAMS
Prahran
HIGH
Armadale
GLENFERRIE
STREET
DANDENONG ROAD
Alma Park
Malvern
PRINCES HIGHWAY
HIGH STREET
INKERMAN STREET
St. Kilda
CARLISLE STREET
BALACLAVA ROAD
BRIGHTON ROAD
St. Kilda East
HOTHAM STREET
ORONG ROAD
Caulfield North
Caulfield Racecourse
Luna Park
Rippon Lea
Point Ormond
Elwood
Elsternwick

0   1   2 km
0   1 mile

AREAS OF THE CITY

On Sundays an open-air arts and craft market, along the Esplanade, sells hand-crafted goods, some of which are very unusual and original (open 09.00–17.00 hrs).

The most colourful feature of St Kilda is its best known landmark—**Luna Park**. The city's amusement park has been on the site since 1912, and among its many attractions is a carousel which dates back to the park's earliest days, and is still a great favourite.

South Melbourne, nearly two miles (3km) south of the city and once called Emerald Hill, was a huge camping area in the 1850s, following the discovery of gold in Victoria. Thousands who flocked to the goldfields stayed in this temporary canvas town, and more than 30 hotels, built during those boom years, are still open.

South Yarra is a fashionable suburb with a floating population of young people. There are good shops and restaurants, and this is a popular place for shopping and window-shopping, especially at weekends.

Toorak, three miles (5km) southeast of the city, is synonymous with wealth. This is where the families of old built their palatial mansions. It is a beautiful suburb, with winding tree-lined streets, a shopping area (called a 'village'), mock Tudor buildings and small arcades.

Williamstown, eight miles (13km) west of the city, is a bayside suburb which has been 're-discovered' recently, and has retained its old maritime atmosphere. The quickest way there is to drive over the West Gate Bridge.

Luna Park is nearly 80 years old, but its appeal is timeless

WHAT TO SEE

Buildings

The grand façade of the City Baths

◆◆
THE AUSTRALIAN AND NEW ZEALAND (ANZ) BANK AND ANZ BANKING MUSEUM
386 Collins Street
Even if you do not want to do any banking, do walk into this bank. It is a quite unique, highly decorated Venetian gothic revival-style building, with little balconies, which has been compared with the Doge's Palace in Venice. Its interior is magnificent, in blue tones with gold leaf ornamentation amid graceful arches and pillars. Formerly the England, Scottish and Australian Bank, the building displays decorative shields of those countries and other cities throughout the world where the original bank traded. This is considered the finest secular example of gothic revival-style architecture in Australia. It was designed by William Wardell and made of sandstone from Sydney, New South Wales. On the lower ground floor a museum presents changing exhibitions illustrating the history of Australian banking (tel: 607 4305).

◆
CITY BATHS
420 Swanston Street
The City Baths, which include swimming pools and private baths, are housed within an eye-catching building which has won awards for restoration. Built in 1903, it fell into disrepair over the years and was in danger of being demolished; but it was rescued, renovated and re-opened in 1983, with modern amenities included. There are six squash courts, a fully equipped gymnasium, spas and saunas, lounges and a solarium. *Open:* Monday to Friday 06.15–22.00 hrs; Saturday, Sunday and Public Holidays 08.00–18.00 hrs.

◆◆◆
COMO HOUSE
Como Avenue, South Yarra
This elegant home, owned by

WHAT TO SEE

the National Trust, is set amid beautifully landscaped gardens, and personifies the gracious way of life of Melbourne soon after the city was founded. The kitchen out-building dates back to the 1840s; the original laundry and some of the original furnishings also remain. Balls held here were the highlight of the social calendar. It was the home of the Armytage family for 95 years from 1864.
Open: daily, 10.00–17.00 hrs. Closed Good Friday and Christmas Day. Admission charge. Guided tours available. Tram 8 from Swanston Street to stop 30.

◆
GOVERNMENT HOUSE
Dallas Brooks Drive, King's Domain
Government House is the official residence of the Governor of Victoria, the Queen's representative in Victoria. Royalty and other heads of state stay here when on official visits to Melbourne. Set within quiet gardens, with the city skyline above the trees, this imposing mansion was built in 1876, and its tall tower can be seen from many parts of Melbourne. It boasts a grand ballroom larger than the one in Buckingham Palace!

Como House was the place to be seen in its high society days

Guided tours, organised by the National Trust, can include Victoria's first Government House, which is near by. Tours only; tel: 654 4711.

LA TROBE'S COTTAGE
Birdwood Avenue, King's Domain, near Royal Botanic Gardens
This pretty little cottage was Victoria's first Government House. It was a pre-fabricated house, brought from England to Australia in 1839 by Charles La Trobe, who was to become the first Lieutenant-Governor (in effect the first Governor) of Victoria in 1851. The cottage was at first set up in Jolimont, but has been restored and re-erected on its present site by the National Trust. The furnishings are mostly original.
Open: usually daily, 11.00–16.30 hrs (except Friday), but times vary: it is advisable to check first (tel: 654 5528).

LAW COURTS
Lonsdale Street
These buildings, which include the Supreme Court, are very grand. You can walk through and see the old cobbled courtyards. Above the entrance is the Figure of Justice, and it is interesting to note that, unlike similar figures elsewhere, she does not wear the traditional blindfold. The courts are open to the public during most sittings from 10.00 hrs.

OLD MELBOURNE GAOL
Russell Street (opposite Victorian Police Station)

This is a grim place, full of gloom and doom, with its thick walls, small cells and heavy doors. The only ray of light is a shaft of sun across the remand yard.
The gaol was begun in 1841, and there were two executions even while it was being built. Altogether, there were 104 hangings of men and women here; the death masks of some of them are on display. The most famous is that of bushranger, Ned Kelly, who was hanged on 11 November 1889.
This remaining cell block of the former large gaol dates back to 1851. The gaol was officially closed in 1929 and used for storage, but in 1941 it was re-opened and used as a military prison during World War II.
Open: daily, 09.30–16.30 hrs. Closed Christmas Day and Good Friday. Admission charge.

PARLIAMENT HOUSE
Spring Street, facing Bourke Street
Parliament House is the most dominant and grandest building in Spring Street, with its wide flight of bluestone steps leading up to the entrance. There are beautiful old lamps outside, and the doors are wonderfully carved, shown to good effect by spotlights at night, which also point up the towering Doric columns. It was built in stages from 1854 to 1892—and it is still not finished. There have long been plans for a north and south wing and a dome to be built over the vestibule. But jet-age costs might be prohibitive for these old-time Victorian ideas!
It is very worthwhile walking up

WHAT TO SEE

Keeping Parliament out of the dark

Cathedral (see page 28). The formal opening of the Victorian Parliament took place in 1856. It moved temporarily to the Exhibition Building in 1901, when Parliament House was used as the Australian (Federal) Parliament, from the declaration of Federation in 1901 until Canberra was built as the capital of Australia in 1927. The two chambers were the first sections of the building to be completed. Members of the public can attend sessions of Parliament in the Public Galleries, even late at night or in the early morning, if Members are sitting until then. Parliament sits on Tuesdays, Wednesdays and Thursdays. When Parliament is not sitting, there are guided tours: Monday to Friday 10.00; 11.00; 14.00 and 15.00 hrs. Admission free.

the steep, front steps to view the grandeur of the building's classic interior, with its soaring columns, magnificent ceilings decorated with gold leaf and Waterford chandeliers. Poet John Betjeman described the Legislative Council as 'the best Corinthian room in the world'. It has a Tudor Rose ceiling, and the benches in the two Chambers follow the colours of the British Houses of Parliament: green for the Assembly, as in the House of Commons, red in the Council, as in the House of Lords. In the beautifully galleried library, there are little open fireplaces set into the base of some of the columns; they were used for warming the room in the early days. Through the central windows you can see the most perfect view of St Patrick's

RIPPON LEA
192 Hotham Street, Elsternwick
Rippon Lea is one of Australia's last great suburban properties to remain intact from the Victorian era. The house was built between 1868 and 1887 and has been renovated over the years. It is in ornate Romanesque style, featuring polychrome brickwork, which is multi-coloured and patterned, and was fashionable at the time. The interior is lavish and opulent and is being gradually refurbished. But the main feature is the gardens, spread over 14 acres (5.6 hectares) and superb for meandering. They are full of surprises: there is a fernery, orchard, rose garden, glades, a desert garden with cacti, an ornamental lake with little

islands lined by decorative bridges, a romantic latticed boatshed and banks of flowers (whatever the season, there is always some flower in bloom). Beautifully illustrated booklets on both the house and garden are sold on the premises.
Open: daily, 10.00–17.00 hrs. Closed Christmas Day. Admission charge.
Bus 602 from Queen Street, City to stop 45.

TREASURY BUILDING
at the corner of Spring Street and Treasury Place
The Treasury Building, at the top end of Collins Street and adjacent to the Treasury Gardens, is a superb example of neo-classic architecture. It is one of the finest buildings in Melbourne, designed by a 19-year-old, JJ Clarke, who was a government architect when he designed it, as his first project. He went on to become one of the leading architects of the day. The Treasury was built between 1858 and 1862 and is used for Government offices.
Near by is a triangular reserve, called **Gordon Reserve**, where there are two statues of two Gordons. One is of General Charles Gordon (1833–85), defender of Khartoum. The other is of Adam Lindsay Gordon (1833–70), one of Australia's best-loved poets. Underneath the seat on which he rests is a saddle, denoting his other love, horse-riding. Beside him is a lovely fountain, carved by a prisoner who was serving a gaol sentence for an armed robbery and horse stealing. It took him

two years to complete the fountain and he was released in 1871 and helped to erect it.

UNIVERSITY OF MELBOURNE
Grattan Street, Parkville
Melbourne's university was opened in 1855 and set in attractive grounds, where you can wander around and look at the college buildings—such as Newman College, designed by Walter Burnley Griffin, who designed Australia's capital city, Canberra; or the gothic tower of Ormond College, which can be seen from Royal Park. During the academic year, you can go to public lectures, free lunchtime concerts or concerts in the evening at the beautifully renovated Melba Hall.
The main university vacations are in January and February. There are booklets on walking tours of the university available from the university's Media Office (tel: 344 7081).
The Media Office is open from Monday to Friday 10.00–16.00 hrs.

Churches

COLLINS STREET CHURCHES
Collins Street
On two opposite corners of Russell Street and Collins Street are two striking looking churches. The **Uniting Church**, formerly the Independent Church, is an 1866 Tuscan-style building with a tall tower. It replaces an 1838 wooden chapel, which was the first church built in the colony of Victoria. The present church features 19 stained glass

windows and inside there is an unusual gallery and cast-iron balustrade under a domed ceiling (tours: Monday to Friday at 11.30 hrs).

Scots Church was a simple building when first opened, but through the generosity of some of its members, who became wealthy in the gold era, the gothic-style embellishments were added in 1841.

Further down the street is the **Collins Street Baptist Church**, Australia's oldest Baptist church building. The present church, opened in 1862, is a great contrast to the many gothic revival-style 19th-century buildings in Melbourne. It is a beautiful, cream-coloured church, which looks like a temple, with its classic parapet and portico of four Corinthian columns.

◆
ST FRANCIS' CHURCH
312 Lonsdale Street
On the corner of Elizabeth Street and Lonsdale Street is the Roman Catholic Church of St Francis. Its foundation stone was laid in 1841, and it is the oldest building in Melbourne still standing on its original site and serving its original purpose. Today it is dwarfed by gleaming glass edifices, but it is a much-loved church, busy during the day with office workers and shoppers attending day-time Masses and other services. It is estimated that 10,000 people visit it weekly.

◆
ST JAMES' OLD CATHEDRAL
King Street, at the corner of Batman Street

Across the road from the Flagstaff Gardens (see page 36), this delightful little church is the oldest in Melbourne; building was begun in 1839. It was originally situated at the corner of Little Collins and William Streets, but was moved stone by stone to its present site in 1913.

ST PATRICK'S CATHEDRAL
Cathedral Place, East Melbourne
The graceful spires of the bluestone St Patrick's Roman Catholic Cathedral, the tallest in Melbourne, are seen from many points around the city. They were added between 1937 and 1939 to the early gothic-style cathedral, which was completed in 1897. The highest of the three spires is 340 feet (103m).
The interior of St Patrick's soars with magnificent, slender pillars. Noteworthy features include the large stained glass windows, the floor mosaics and the exquisite glass mosaics, made in Venice, which are set into the marble and alabaster altars.
Open: Monday to Friday 07.00–18.00 hrs; Saturday 07.00–20.00 hrs; Sunday 08.00–19.30 hrs.
Tram 9, 10, 11, 12 or 42 from Collins Street to stop 15.

ST PAUL'S CATHEDRAL
at the corner of Swanston and Flinders Streets
The lovely warm stone of St Paul's Cathedral, with its lofty spires and towers and trees, gives it an air of calm, as it stands at this busy intersection. It was on this site, once a corn and hay market, that Melbourne's first

official church service was held in 1836. The cathedral was started in 1880 and completed in 1931. Its interior features superb stained glass windows and lovely cedar woodwork carved in gothic style. On Wednesday evenings the peals of bells ringing out over the traffic's noise signals practice time for the bell ringers, preparing for Sunday services.

ST PETER'S CHURCH
469 Albert Street, Eastern Hill
This is Melbourne's parish church, and is one of the oldest and prettiest of the city's churches. It stands opposite the grand St Patrick's Cathedral in a little churchyard all of its own, and has been the site of some historic occasions since its foundation stone was laid by Governor La Trobe in 1846. It was here that Bishop Perry was received as Melbourne's first Anglican Bishop, and from the church steps, Melbourne was proclaimed a city.

Galleries and Museums

AUSTRALIAN CENTRE FOR CONTEMPORARY ART
Dallas Brooks Drive, South Yarra
Temporary exhibitions of both Australian and international artists.
Open: Tuesday to Friday 10.30–17.00 hrs; Saturday and Sunday 14.00–17.00 hrs.

AUSTRALIAN GALLERY OF SPORT
Jolimont
Comprehensive coverage of about 20 major sports; using

St Paul's soars above the traffic

permanent and temporary exhibitions, memorabilia and audio-visuals. It includes an Olympic Museum with exhibits from the first modern Olympics, held in Athens in 1896.
Open: Tuesday to Sunday 10.00–16.00 hrs; closed Monday. Admission charge.
The museum is at the **Melbourne Cricket Ground**, which also features a Cricket Club Museum and gives a two-hour guided tour of the museum and ground on Wednesdays at 10.00 hrs.

HEIDE PARK AND ART GALLERY
7 Templestowe Road, Bulleen

WHAT TO SEE

This is a delightful place, set on the banks of the Yarra River. The property was bought in 1934 by John and Sunday Reed, who were great lovers of art. It was a run-down dairy farm, and the Reeds created an environment for artists to meet and work, and built a contemporary home, which is now the gallery, with a permanent collection (temporary exhibitions are also held). There are attractive grounds, which have some contemporary sculpture.
Open: Tuesday to Friday 10.00–17.00 hrs; Saturdays and Sundays 12.00–17.00 hrs. Admission charge.

◆
LEONE RYAN'S HALL OF AUSTRALIAN BUSH LIFE
Banana Alley, Flinders Street
Towards Spencer Street Railway Station is a row of restored, 100-year-old vaults, built by the railways and used to store bananas. This is now called Banana Alley, and the vaults house, as well as wine cellars and shops, a unique exhibition, which is the work of one woman. Leone Ryan's Hall of Australian Bush Life, at vaults 1 and 2, portrays everyday scenes of life in the outback with figures modelled in clay, which took her 12 years to complete. There are 70 different scenes, 7,000 pieces: farmers droving sheep and cattle and horses, a shearing shed scene, the country in drought, horse and bullock teams pulling bales of wool and wheat. There are animals and birds, kangaroos, dogs, snakes, goannas, parrots, cockatoos. All these are made out of clay and

Australian bush crafts in Banana Alley's 100-year-old vaults

other materials from the bush. Gum leaves burn, giving the air the authentic scent of the bush. You can have a cup of tea while you are chatting to Leone, who works on the family farm, mustering and drenching cattle and sheep. Her family has worked on the land for five generations.

Open: Tuesday to Sunday 10.00–16.00 hrs; closed Mondays (except Public Holidays), Christmas Day and Good Friday. Children must be accompanied by adults. Admission charge.

THE MEAT MARKET CRAFT CENTRE
42 Courtney Street, North Melbourne
This centre houses the Victorian State craft collection, and works from the collection are on display and changed at regular intervals. Crafts include ceramics, woodcraft, textiles, jewellery and glass, which is especially innovative in design and colour. Resident craftspeople work at the centre, and there are items for sale. The building, dating back to the 1880s, was one of the city's largest meat markets.
Open: Monday to Sunday 10.00–17.00 hrs. Admission free.

MELBOURNE FIRE BRIGADE MUSEUM
48 Gisborne Street, corner of Victoria Parade, East Melbourne
There is a fascinating array of fire brigade memorabilia in this museum. It includes old fire engines, still a gleaming red, fire extinguishers, a wonderful display of helmets and some

quite dashing 18th-century uniforms, which were once used by insurance company firemen. There is also a collection of model fire engines. The museum is housed in a red-brick building, completed in 1893 and used as the Headquarters of the Metropolitan Fire Brigade for 87 years. Its tall tower was used as a lookout point for fires as late as the 1970s. The present Fire Brigade Headquarters is next door, and the modern fire engines can be seen through glass doors. On the corner of the building, the grey surface is highlighted by a huge, brightly coloured mural, portraying 'The Legend of Fire'. It took one-and-a-half years to complete and one million glass mosaic tiles were used.
Open: Friday 09.00–15.00 hrs; Sunday 10.00–16.00 hrs. Other times by application to the secretary (tel: 665 4249). Admission charge. Children under four free.

MELBOURNE MARITIME MUSEUM
corner of Normanby and Phayer Streets, South Melbourne
The centrepiece of this museum is the *Polly Woodside*, a commercial sailing ship built in Belfast in 1885. It was on the South American run and went around Cape Horn 16 times. For 20 years from 1904 it sailed between the Pacific and Australia, before being converted to a coal hulk in 1923. By 1962 this was the last sailing ship still afloat in Australia. Beautifully restored, the *Polly Woodside* is moored afloat at an

old dock site. The museum also has other sailing exhibits.
Open: Monday to Friday 10.00–16.00 hrs; Saturday and Sunday 12.00–17.00 hrs. Closed Good Friday and Christmas Day. Admission charge.

MUSEUM OF CHINESE AUSTRALIAN HISTORY
22–24 Cohen Place
Set in Cohen Place, which is fronted by a Chinese gate and two traditional stone lions, the museum has some excellent exhibits and an interesting audio-visual presentation tracing the history of the Chinese in Victoria. Exhibits include a life-size replica of a Warrior General from the 2nd century BC—the only such replica outside the People's Republic of China; a *cloisonné* seismograph which measured earthquakes many years ago and Dai Loong, the largest ceremonial dragon in the world, 330 feet (100m) long, who is 'awakened' for Chinese New Year celebrations and the Moomba Parade, when it parades through the streets propelled by 100 legs (belonging to 50 men!).
Chinese Heritage Walks are organised by the Chinese Museum during February and March. They include a guided tour of the museum, a walk through Little Bourke Street, a visit to a Chinese herbalist, *yum cha* at a Chinese restaurant and a demonstration of Chinese music, dance, *tai chi* or painting.
Open: Monday to Thursday 10.00–17.00 hrs; weekends, 12.00–17.00 hrs. Admission charge.

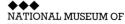

NATIONAL MUSEUM OF VICTORIA
328 Swanston Street
Impressive exhibits of the history of Melbourne are housed here, tracing the discovery of gold in Victoria and the country's environment (with the help of some live ants and snakes). Impressive natural history and science displays include Australia's first car and plane and the body of the legendary racehorse Phar Lap (see **Sport**, page 102).
Open: daily, 10.00–17.00 hrs. Admission free.
The **Children's Museum** (admission free) and the **Planetarium** (admission charge) are within the museum.
Also within the museum building is the **State Library**, with its domed reading room and more than a million books and newspapers. **La Trobe Library** (entrance from La Trobe Street) features Australiana; and there are some excellent temporary exhibitions displaying archival material.
Open: Monday to Friday 10.00–22.00 hrs (until 18.00 hrs at weekends).

VICTORIAN ARTISTS' SOCIETY
430 Albert Street, East Melbourne
The Victorian Artists' Society, the oldest artists' society in Australia, was established in 1870 and held its first exhibition in the present galleries. This is a charming building, with a lovely centre staircase leading to upper galleries. There are always exhibitions of paintings,

Reaching the heights of excellence: the Victorian Arts Centre

sculpture and drawings by contemporary artists. These and unframed works are for sale. If you happen to be there in February, there is a bargain sale of sketches, drawings and paintings.
Open: Monday to Friday 10.00–17.00 hrs. Admission free.

◆◆◆
THE VICTORIAN ARTS CENTRE
St Kilda Road
Across Princes Bridge, on the south bank of the Yarra River, you leave behind the bustle of the commercial side of the city and come into the quiet of parklands and the Arts Centre complex. Within the walls of

these buildings the main works of art, concerts, opera, ballet and theatres of Melbourne are housed.
The Arts Centre is the heart of Melbourne's culture. The complex includes the National Gallery of Victoria, the Melbourne Concert Hall, the Performing Arts Museum and the Theatres building, where the theatres are six levels below St Kilda Road. The 377-foot (115m) spire which tops the Centre is a Melbourne landmark, especially when illuminated at night. This has created an added attraction —hundreds of seagulls fly

around the lights, attracted by insects.

The National Gallery, 180 St Kilda Road, is the oldest building in the complex, completed in 1968 (the others were built in the 1980s). There are more than 70,000 works of arts, ranging from 2400BC to the present and including pre-Columbian art, Aboriginal, European Old Masters and American, as well as costumes, textiles and a wonderful glass collection. Tiepolo, Rembrandt, Picasso, Rodin and Henry Moore are featured, as is a superb collection of Australian artists. Pools run the length of the four-storey, bluestone building, and in the water stands a sculpture you could not miss: a two-headed, three-legged mythological angel by Deborah Halpern. It stands 32 feet (10m) tall, is made of steel, concrete and ceramics, and is covered with hand-painted, colourfully glazed tiles. A brilliant feature in the Great Hall is the glass ceiling made by Australian artist Leonard French: a kaleidoscope of rich red, green and blue, dazzling under the sun's rays. *Open:* daily, 10.00–17.00 hrs. Closed Monday, except on public holidays. Admission charge.

In the **Performing Arts Museum** over a quarter of a million items about the theatre include a collection of memorabilia associated with Dame Nellie Melba, the singer who was born and took her name from the city. *Open:* Monday to Saturday 11.00–18.00 hrs; Sunday noon–18.00 hrs. Admission charge.

There are guided tours of the concert hall and theatres (see **Nightlife and Entertainment**, page 89) lasting one hour and leaving from the Concert Hall (St Kilda Road level) at the following times: Monday to Friday 10.30, 12.00, 13.15 and 14.30 hrs; Saturday 10.30 and 12.00 hrs; Sunday 11.15, 12.30, 13.45 and 15.00 hrs. Admission charge.

◆
VICTORIAN TAPESTRY WORKSHOP
260 Park Street, South Melbourne
This is one of the few great tapestry workshops in the world, established in 1976 and able to undertake the weaving by hand of large-scale tapestries for architectural locations. Designs for the tapestries are created by some of the foremost Australian contemporary artists: Arthur Boyd, John Olsen and John Coburn; and the weavers are all artists in their own right. Some of the original designs have incorporated all manner of materials—prints, photographs, letters and documents.

The workshop is within a light and airy Victorian building, a former emporium of the 19th century, and several tapestries are generally being woven at one time, all at different stages. Many of the completed tapestries hang in public places throughout Australia and overseas. The largest to date was the tapestry designed by Arthur Boyd for the Great Hall of the new Parliament House in Canberra. It measures 65 by 29 feet (20 by 9m) and took 12 weavers two years to complete.

It is believed to be the largest tapestry in the world produced this century. Two tapestries produced by the workshop are near the entrance to the Regent Hotel in Collins Street. They represent the floral symbols of Australia and Victoria: the golden wattle and pink heath. Weavers can be seen at work through the window of an adjoining studio. You can also visit the workshop, by appointment only (tel: 699 7885). *Viewing:* Tuesday, Wednesday, Thursday at 14.00 and 14.30 hrs.

Commercial galleries include: **Australian Galleries**, 35 Derby Street, Collingwood, which mostly exhibits established artists; **Gallery Gabrielle Pizzi**, 141 Flinders Lane, City, specialising in Aboriginal art; **Gould Galleries**, 270 Toorak Road, South Yarra, which exhibits work of prominent Australian painter Greg Irvine; **Tolarno**, 98 River Street, South Yarra, established by Georges Mora; and his son's, **William Mora Galleries**, 19 Windsor Place, City; the Mora name is well known in art circles.

Parks and Gardens
Melbourne is awash, on either side of the Yarra River, with parks and gardens. They were planned in the early days of the city, and most are within easy walking distance or a short tram ride from the city's centre.

CARLTON GARDENS
Nicholson Street, at the northern end of Spring Street
In the centre of these gardens, more popularly known as the Exhibition Gardens, is the **Royal Exhibition Building**, built for the Great Exhibition of 1880 by

A Victorian monument to civic pride – the Royal Exhibition Building

WHAT TO SEE

David Mitchell, Dame Nellie Melba's father. It is used today for commercial exhibitions.
If you walk alongside the gardens, along Nicholson Street, you will come to a beautifully restored row of terrace houses, **Royal Terrace**, which was built in the 1850s of bluestone, and is one of Melbourne's oldest. Around the corner in Gertrude Street are the more recently restored façades of **Glass Terrace**, built around the same time.
Tram 86, 88, 96 or 111 from Bourke Street to stop 10.

◆◆◆
FITZROY AND TREASURY GARDENS
bordered by Spring, Wellington, Clarendon, Albert and Lansdowne Streets
The Treasury Gardens edge on to the city at the top end of Collins Street, overlooked by the Treasury Building, and are popular with office workers during the lunch break. There are elms, oaks, poplars and plane trees, an ornamental lake, and a memorial to President John F Kennedy. The gardens are the setting for an outdoor art show held during the Moomba festival in March. Adjoining the Treasury Gardens are the Fitzroy Gardens, with magnificent avenues of elms forming canopies across the pathways, and partly hidden glades and waterfalls set off the main pathways.
Cook's Cottage, the home of Captain James Cook's parents, was bought at auction on its Yorkshire site in England, and re-erected in Melbourne in 1934,

having been shipped to Australia in 253 cases and 40 barrels. This small, pretty cottage dates back to 1755. Only 15 people are allowed into the cottage at one time. In the stable there is an interesting pictorial history of Captain Cook and his voyages of discovery (open daily, 09.00 – 17.00 hrs; admission charge).
Also in the gardens is a **Fairy Tree**, carved with fantasy figures and Australian animals by sculptress Ola Cohn; and a **miniature Tudor village**, presented to Melbourne by the people of Lambeth, London, in appreciation of food parcels sent to Britain after World War II.

◆
FLAGSTAFF GARDENS
bordered by King, William and La Trobe Streets, West Melbourne
In the early days the high, sloping ground of these gardens made them ideal as an observation point to watch ships coming into Port Phillip Bay. The land was used as a signalling station, complete with flagstaff, and as a burial ground for the early settlers. Established in 1840, it is one of the city's oldest gardens; today it is landscaped with trees and flowers.

◆◆◆
KING'S DOMAIN, ALEXANDRA GARDENS AND THE QUEEN VICTORIA GARDENS
access off St Kilda Road, via Princes Bridge
These regally named gardens adjoin the Royal Botanic Gardens (see page 37), making a continuous parkland from Princes Bridge to South Yarra.

Alexandra Avenue runs through the parklands, which cover 529 acres (214 hectares). Features include a statue of Queen Victoria, delicate sculptures of women and children, and a floral clock, whose design and flowers are changed throughout the year. The clock was presented to Melbourne in 1966 by the watchmakers of Switzerland. The **Sidney Myer Music Bowl** is an open-air venue for both classical and pop concerts. Near the Royal Botanic Gardens is the **Shrine of Remembrance**, a memorial to Victorian servicemen and women who died in wartime. Within the shrine, the stone of remembrance is set into the floor, positioned so that at 11 o'clock on 11 November (Armistice Day) a ray of sunlight passes over it. The Shrine is the focal point for services on Anzac Day (25 April), when those who died in the wars are remembered. There is a simple ceremony as dawn breaks over the city, and later in the day ex-servicemen and women march through the city streets to the Shrine.

There is an observation deck affording panoramic views of the city, parklands and Port Phillip Bay (open Monday to Saturday 10.00–17.00 hrs).

◆
MELBOURNE GENERAL CEMETERY
College Crescent, Parkville
This was one of the first cemeteries in the world to be divided into denominational sections. The earliest graves date back to 1853, and one of the

The tranquil Royal Botanic Gardens

founding fathers of Melbourne, John Pascoe Fawkner, is buried here. A more unexpected memorial, but to a person known more internationally, is that of Elvis Presley. Fans of 'the King' visit the memorial on his birthday, 8 January, each year. *Open:* daily, 08.00–17.00 hrs. Guided tours: The Necropolis (tel: 546 9377). Tram 1 or 15 from Swanston Street to stop 15.

◆◆◆
ROYAL BOTANIC GARDENS
Birdwood Avenue (adjoining King's Domain), Alexandra

WHAT TO SEE

Tribute is paid to those who died in the war at the Shrine of Remembrance

Avenue and Anderson Street, South Yarra
These are acclaimed as one of the finest gardens in the world. They cover around 88 acres (35 hectares) and were superbly landscaped more than 100 years ago, by William Guilfoyle. Famous botanist Baron von Mueller established the gardens in 1846, and they now boast more than 12,000 species of plants from around the world. These are gardens for all seasons: camellias are best from June to August, blossom from August to October and rhododendrons and azaleas from September to November.

In summer there are open-air re-enactments in different venues around the gardens of such stories as *The Wind in the Willows, Alice's Adventures in Wonderland* and *A Midsummer Night's Dream* (tel: 663 8307 for information); there are also free guided walks through the gardens, 10.00–11.00 hrs each day, except Mondays and Saturdays. Groups of six or more must book (tel: 650 9424). Admission to the park is free; the gates close at sunset.
Open: from 07.00 or 07.30 hrs in the summer months; 08.30 or 09.00 hrs during winter.
Tram 8 from Swanston Street to stop 21.

◆◆◆
THE ROYAL MELBOURNE ZOOLOGICAL GARDENS
Elliott Avenue, Parkville
On a quiet night in Parkville, you can hear the roar of lions from the zoo, which has been acclaimed as one of the finest in the world. It is also one of the oldest in the world, opened in 1857, and now housing more than 3,000 animals, including a variety of Australian species, such as kangaroos, koalas, emus, wombats, seals and bandicoots, mainly living in open landscaped

enclosures. When you walk through the lions' den, you are the one in the caged bridge! You can walk through the **Butterfly House** and the **Great Flight Aviary**, a natural setting of trees and pools, which is home to hundreds of birds.

Open: daily, 09.00–17.00 hrs. Admission charge. Friends of the Zoo provide free guided tours, which are available from Monday to Friday 10.00–14.00 hrs; weekends 11.00–15.00 hrs.

Tram 55 or 56 from William Street from Monday to Saturday. Sundays only: tram 68 travels from Elizabeth Street to stop 21. Vintage trams also operate on Sundays at regular intervals from Elizabeth Street.

The zoo is within **Royal Park**, and is its main attraction. Set within the leafy tree-shaded streets this is the largest park in Melbourne, covering 444 acres (180 hectares). It has a country atmosphere about it, with wide open spaces planted with a wonderful variety of gum trees. Some lose their bark, leaving limbs that are beautifully smooth and unblemished. There is an attractively landscaped area, with a pond offset by rushes, and facilities include cricket and football fields, public tennis courts and a golf course.

Trams

Melbourne is the only city in Australia which has retained its trams. There has been a tramway system here for more than 100 years; there are now more than 700 trams. Most are painted green and cream (the famous 'green rattlers') and some

are works of art, painted by well-known Victorian artists in their own individual styles. One unique tram is the **Colonial Tramcar Restaurant**, which travels on a scenic route around Melbourne while you wine and dine (tel: 596 6500).

Trams have numbers which indicate their route; stops are clearly marked—either at the side or in the middle of the street—and numbered, which makes it easy to find your destination. Normal hours of operation are 05.00–midnight, Monday to Friday, with reduced services at weekends and holidays.

The principal services operate from Swanston and Elizabeth Streets (north and south); Flinders, Collins and Bourke Streets and Batman Avenue (east and west), with buses providing additional services (see **Directory**, under **Public Transport**).

There are a few particularly scenic routes, which you can enjoy simply as a means of sightseeing.

Tram 8, from Swanston Street to Glenferrie Road, takes you to the South Yarra and Toorak shopping centres, to Chapel Street and to historic Como House. It is a beautiful route, passing ornate terrace houses with tiny balconies and statuary, on Park Street; St Kilda Road, once lined with mansions, now the setting for luxurious apartments and offices; the large, leafy Fawkner Park, and Toorak Village, which is only the length of two tram stops (32 and 33). Sometimes tram 8 does not terminate at Glenferrie Road, but returns to the Tram Depot. If this is the case, it will turn right into Glenferrie Road at the terminus, and you can stay on until you come to the Malvern Town Hall, an elegant white building.

Tram 6, which travels along High Street, to the right of the Town Hall, takes you back to the city, going along St Kilda Road and finishing in Swanston Street, as does Tram 8.

Tram 15, from Swanston Street to St Kilda, is a good tram to take on a Sunday, when the arts and crafts market is open along the Esplanade.

On the way there, at St Kilda Junction, the tram turns into Fitzroy Street; at the bottom you will see Port Phillip Bay. The tram terminates near the big face of Luna Park. Across the road is Acland Street, renowned for its Middle European atmosphere.

As an alternative to the trams, **bus 605**, from Batman Avenue, near Princes Bridge has the prettiest view of the Yarra River possible by public transport. You need go only as far as Toorak Village; the return trip is even more scenic, as you also have a beautiful view of the city skyline. If possible, sit on the right-hand side of the bus, and on the left on the return journey. The short trip takes you across Morell Bridge, at Anderson Street, with its decorative iron railings and old lampposts. Look out for the Rialto, tallest of the high-rise city buildings, which changes colours in the varying natural light. At Punt Road, look to the right to see one of the most beautiful single trees in Melbourne: a large golden elm, whose branches bow to the ground in a vast canopy.

If you extend your trip a little further than Toorak Village, you will pass through narrow back streets with delightful old houses and gardens until you come to High Street, Armadale, noted for its antique and other shops.

Enjoyable and fumeless travel: trams rattle along Collins Street

EXCURSIONS FROM MELBOURNE

◆◆◆
BALLARAT

seventy miles (113km) from Melbourne

Ballarat is Victoria's largest inland city and one of the major gold towns of the past. Galleries, museums, and antique and craft shops are dotted about the town. The **City of Ballarat Fine Art Gallery**, 40 Lydiard Street North, has a fine collection of Australian paintings from the Colonial and Heidelberg Schools (open Tuesday to Friday 10.30–16.30 hrs; Saturday, Sunday and public holidays 12.30–16.30 hrs; closed Mondays, Good Friday and Christmas Day). A shuttlebus service runs to all major attractions; there is also a sightseeing tram.

Sovereign Hill, at the corner of Main Road and Bradshaw Street, in Ballarat, is a superb re-creation of a gold town of the 1850s. People dressed in the costume of the day go about their work, and visitors can walk along the main street, go to the shops or the theatre, and see craftsmen at work. Walk into one of the cottages and you might be in time for some freshly baked scones! There is a school with pupils being taught in the old style, and you can even pan for gold. (Open daily, 09.30–17.00 hrs; closed Christmas Day. Admission charge).

Montrose Cottage and Eureka Museum, 111 Eureka Street, is Ballarat's last original miners' bluestone cottage, built in 1856. The small museum houses an interesting collection of

Ballarat today is a gold mine of gardens, shops and museums

domestic and mining items from 1850 to the early 20th century. (Open daily, 09.30–17.00 hrs. Admission charge).

◆◆
BEECHWORTH

nearly 170 miles (271km) from Melbourne

Beechworth had one of Australia's richest goldfields, but today the soft golden glow about the town comes from the honey-coloured granite of its restored old buildings, 32 of which are classified by the National Trust as 'historically important'. The gaol has held some famous prisoners including Ned Kelly, who was held twice!

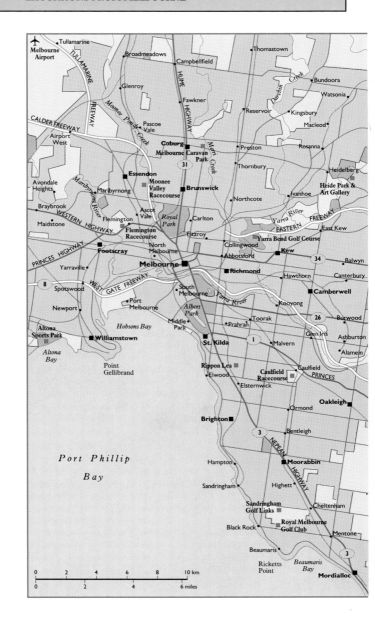

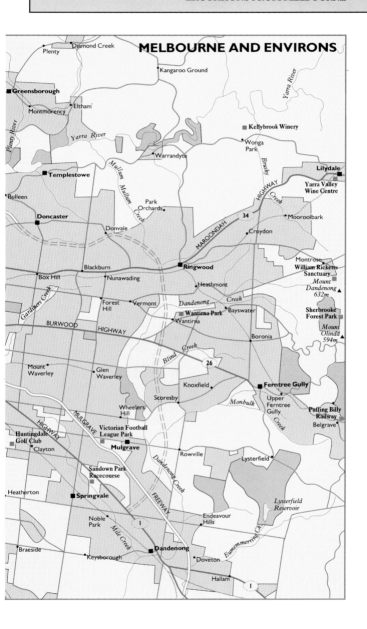

MELBOURNE AND ENVIRONS

EXCURSIONS FROM MELBOURNE

◆◆◆
BENDIGO

91 miles (150km) from Melbourne

Bendigo is another gold city of old. Its attractions include the **Central Deborah Gold Mine** and **Bendigo Art Gallery**. At the **Bendigo Mohair Farm**, Maryborough Road, Lockwood (tel: (054) 35 3225), you can see mohair products being made (open daily from 10.00 hrs). Other places on the drive from Melbourne include **Mount Macedon**, 37 miles (61km) from Melbourne, with beautiful gardens, occasionally open (tel: (054) 26 1561); and **Hanging Rock**, near Woodend, 42 miles (69km) from Melbourne.

◆◆◆
THE DANDENONG RANGES

twenty-one miles (35km) from Melbourne

An hour's drive along a straight highway takes you into another world: forests of soaring mountain ash trees, natural bushland, magnificent gardens and scenic views. Little townships, art galleries and craft shops are tucked away amid the trees, and restaurants range from **Coonara Springs Restaurant**, Coonara Road, Olinda (tel: 751 1043), within a pretty house and garden, to **Burnham Beeches Country House**, Sherbrooke Road, Sherbrooke (tel: 755 1903), grand and expensive.

The **National Rhododendron Gardens**, Falls Road, Olinda (tel: 751 1980), have more than 15,000 rhododendrons and 12,000 azaleas. There are tulip farms,

The Dandenongs offer a wealth of galleries as well as natural beauty

the largest belonging to the
Tesselaar family at Monbulk
Road, Silvan (tel: 737 9305).
William Ricketts Sanctuary,
Mount Dandenong Tourist Road,
Mount Dandenong (tel:
751 1300), is set amid natural
surroundings featuring
sculptures by William Ricketts.

◆
DAYLESFORD/HEPBURN SPRINGS
sixty-eight miles (110km) from Melbourne
There are more than 70 springs
in this area, 'discovered' by early
settlers. A bathhouse complex at
Hepburn Springs offers herbal
mineral water baths; you can
also bottle the natural waters
from pumps (free) or buy the
already bottled variety.
Daylesford and Hepburn Springs
were very popular at the turn of
the century for people 'taking
the waters', and some of the
guesthouses from that era have
been restored, including
Bellinzona Country House, Mair
Road, Hepburn Springs (tel:
(053) 48 2271).

◆
ECHUCA
128 miles (206km) north of Melbourne
Situated on the Murray River at
the confluence of the Campaspe
and Goulburn Rivers, this was
Australia's busiest inland port in
the 1880s—the era of the
riverboat. The town retained its
commercial importance until the
passing of the paddle steamer. It
is a pretty town, with many
historic features, including the
massive Red Gun Wharf. The
Bridge Hotel dates from 1859
and was built by Echuca's

founder, Henry Hopwood. There
are cruises on paddle steamers;
a cruise on the *Canberra* takes
you to the Alambec Auto and
Folk Museum.

THE GREAT OCEAN ROAD
This is one of the great scenic
drives. Officially opened in 1932,
it stretches for 186 miles (300km)
along the coast from Torquay,
passing some of the top surfing
beaches of Victoria, through
attractive townships of Lorne
and Apollo Bay, and **Port
Campbell National Park**, which
has the magnificent Twelve
Apostles, a natural formation of
rocks standing like sentinels.
Loch Ard Gorge is also a
spectacular sight; this is where
the sailing ship *Loch Ard* was
shipwrecked in 1878, with only
two survivors. This stretch of
coastline is beautiful, but was
treacherous for sailing ships.
Portland, further west, is the site
of the first white settlements in
Victoria in 1834.

HEALESVILLE SANCTUARY
*Badger Creek Road, Healesville,
forty miles (65km) from
Melbourne*
This is a must if you want to see
some unique Australian animals
at close quarters. More than 200
species of mammals, birds and
reptiles are housed in as near
natural surroundings as possible.
You will see kangaroos,
wombats, emus, koalas and the
platypus swimming underwater.
There are walk-through aviaries,
a wetlands aviary walkway and a
special Nocturnal House.
Open: daily, 09.00–17.00 hrs.
Admission charge.

EXCURSIONS FROM MELBOURNE

A style of life long gone is recalled in McCrae Homestead

◆
MORNINGTON PENINSULA

It takes over two hours to drive alongside the beaches which stretch from St Kilda to Portsea. In many areas it is very built up with uninteresting houses and shopping areas, but there are some interesting sights to see on the way.

A winding road and a chairlift go up to **Arthur's Seat** for spectacular views of Port Phillip Bay and the Mornington Peninsula. The **Chairlift**, Arthur's Seat Road (tel: (059) 81 0412), is open daily from 11.00 hrs, September to April; weekends and holidays only for the rest of the year. Near the summit is **Seawinds**, a reserve with a beautiful garden and trees planted by former owners Sir Thomas and Lady Travers. **Ashcombe Maze**, Red Hill Road, Shoreham, has both a high hedge maze and a rose maze, along with a pleasant garden and tea rooms (admission charge).

One of the first houses to be built on the Peninsula was **McCrae Homestead**, Charles Street, McCrae, off Nepean Highway (tel: (059) 86 2156). It was built, in 1844, of timber from the surrounding hillside and bricks brought from Melbourne by sea, and though it is now set in a suburban street, it still retains the atmosphere of a bygone era. Another fascinating home is **Mulberry Hill**, Golf Links Road, Baxter (tel: 654 4562), where the late Sir Daryl and Lady Lindsay lived. They were both artists, but Joan Lindsay is best known as the author of the book *Picnic at Hanging Rock*. Their home is much as they left it, with paintings by famous Australian artists on the walls.

The first European settlement in Victoria was at **Sorrento**, in 1803.

It lasted only seven months.
There is an official site, marked
by simple graves of early
settlers at Sullivan's Bay, which is
located off the Nepean Highway
between Blairgowrie and
Sorrento.

A display centre opens on
Saturday and Sunday,
13.00–16.00 hrs.

Portsea, like Sorrento, was once
a busy trading outpost, with
paddle steamers travelling to
Melbourne, carrying the lime
used in the city's early buildings.
Portsea has long been a
weekend retreat for wealthy
Melburnians, whose million-
dollar cliff-top homes are well
hidden along private roads.
Ferries run from Sorrento and
Portsea to **Queenscliff**, which lies
on the Bellarine Peninsula, 64
miles (103km) from Melbourne.
The two peninsulas form the
entrance to Port Phillip Bay. (For
ferry information, tel:
(059) 84 1602.) Originally a
fortress and garrison town,
Queenscliff was protected by a
fort, built in 1884 for fear of a
Russian invasion! There are
panoramic views from the cliffs
of the Rip, the hazardous
entrance to Port Phillip Bay.

THE PENGUIN PARADE

*Phillip Island, 74 miles (120km)
from Melbourne*

This great tourist attraction is a
moving and exciting experience.
Every day at dusk, on
Summerland Beach, hundreds of
little penguins come out of the
water and waddle across the
sand on the way to their burrows
in the sand dunes to rest and
feed their young. You view the

procession from stands, but take
a warm jacket or coat; it is chilly,
even in the summer (for
information, tel: (059) 56 8300).

Vineyards

Victorian wines were being
acclaimed both locally and
internationally for their high
quality more than 100 years ago.
In 1889 a St Huberts wine from
Victoria was awarded the Grand
Prix at the Paris Exposition; and
in the 1890s, at the Vienna
Exhibition, the judges refused to
assess a wine from Bendigo, as
they could not believe that such
good wine could come from the
'colonies'! By 1900 Victoria was
producing 75 per cent of all
Australian wines. In the 1890s,
the vine mite *phyloxera* killed
most of the vines, the economic
situation slumped and Australian
tastes changed from wine to
beer. But in recent years there
has been a renaissance in the
wine industry, and there are now
around 200 vineyards in Victoria.
The northeast, around
Rutherglen, and the northwest of
Victoria are the best-known
areas today, but there are some
vineyards close to Melbourne.

YARRA VALLEY

From the 1880s until 1912, the
Yarra Valley was one of the
largest producing and highest-
quality wine regions in Australia.
Today, again, it is producing
some of the finest wines in
Australia. This was where the
first wine was produced in
Victoria in 1845, and it was here
that the top vintners from
Neuchâtel in Switzerland
established their vineyards.

EXCURSIONS FROM MELBOURNE

The Valley escaped the vine mite, but could not survive changing tastes. The Australian preference for the sweeter wines produced in warmer climates proved disastrous for this valley with its cool climate and light, dry wines. The vines were pulled out and replaced by dairy herds. But in the 1960s vines were again being planted. In 1969 Yeringberg, which had been the last of the 19th-century vineyards to cease commercial production, in 1921, was re-established in a small way (not open to the public).

More than 80 vineyards now flourish in the Valley. Not all are open to the public, but there are many larger ones you can visit, where you can buy wines at the cellar door or take part in tastings. Some wineries are visited by appointment only. Information on the Yarra Valley vineyards is available from the **Yarra Valley Wine Centre**, 1 Maroondah Highway, Lilydale (tel: 739 5089 or 735 1719). They can supply you with maps and will make appointments for you if you want to see a particular vineyard. The Centre is situated near the beginning of the Valley, and is also a private home and restaurant (open for luncheon Thursday, Friday and Sunday from 12.00 hrs; dinner, Wednesday, Thursday, Friday and Saturday from 19.00 hrs). A few of the wineries open to the public are listed below. You will need a car to get to them.

De Bortoli Yarrinya Winery, Pinnacle Lane (off Melba Highway), Dixons Creek, 35 miles (56km) east of Melbourne (tel: (059) 65 2271), is one of the largest vineyards in the Valley. There is a panoramic view from the excellent hillside restaurant, and attractive grounds where it is possible to picnic or cook your own meal on barbecues. Cellar door sales.
Open: Monday to Saturday 09.00–18.00 hrs; Sunday, noon–18.00 hrs.
Restaurant: Luncheon, daily. Dinner, Friday and Saturday.

Domaine Chandon, Green Point, Maroondah Highway, Coldstream (tel: 739 1110). The great champagne producers of France, Moët et Chandon, have established this multi-million dollar vineyard and winery—the company's second winery outside France. The first Domaine Chandon is in the Napa Valley of California, and is the leading producer of premium sparkling wine in the United States.
Telephone for times of tours and tastings.

Fergussons Winery, Wills Road, via Maroondah Highway, Yarra Glen (tel: (059) 65 2237). The original winery and restaurant, established in 1968, were destroyed by fire in 1989; the newly built restaurant opened only eight months later. It is in country style, with hand-crafted wooden tables and benches; spit-roast beef luncheons are a speciality.
Cellar door open: Monday to Saturday 10.00–17.00 hrs; Sunday and public holidays 12.00–18.00 hrs. Tours by appointment.
Restaurant: Luncheon, daily except Monday. Dinner, Thursday to Saturday. Reservations essential.

Kellybrook Winery, Fulford Road, Wonga Park (tel: 722 1304 or 722 1525), is the nearest vineyard to Melbourne, situated in rolling countryside near the Yarra River, 22 miles (35km) east of Melbourne. It has unique ciders, including a *Méthode Champenoise* Champagne Cider, which is delectable. There is a restaurant, with an open fireplace; owner Darren Kelly might sing an Irish song or two!
Cellar door and tastings.
Open: daily, Monday to Saturday 09.00–18.00 hrs; Sunday and public holidays 11.00–18.00 hrs. Closed Boxing Day and New Year's Day.
Restaurant: Luncheon, Saturday and Sunday at 12.30 hrs. Dinner, Friday and Saturday at 19.30 hrs. Other days by arrangement. Booking is essential.
Yarra Burn Vineyards, Settlement Road, Yarra Junction, 40 miles (65km) east of Melbourne (tel: (059) 67 1428), has a magnificent vista of the beautiful Warburton Ranges. The original bluestone winery has been converted into a restaurant. Australian folk songs are often sung and guests are invited to join in.
Cellar door open: Wednesday to Sunday 10.00–17.00 hrs.
Restaurant: Luncheon, Sunday at 13.00 hrs. Dinner, Friday and Saturday at 19.00 hrs. Other nights by arrangement. Wheelchair dining and toilets for the disabled. Reservations are essential.
Yarra Vale Vineyard, Maroondah Highway, Coldstream (tel: (059) 62 5226), has a stunning modern winery

and restaurant set amid the vines. As you walk through the winery you can see the whole process of wine-making through a glass wall.
Cellar door open: daily, 10.00–17.00 hrs.

There are a couple of other vineyards which are situated close to Melbourne. They are about 25 miles (40km) northwest of Melbourne, half an hour's drive from the city and are located opposite each other.
Craiglee Vineyard, Sunbury Road, Sunbury (tel: 744 1160 and 744 4489), was established in 1864, and its original bluestone winery is still standing. Vines were pulled out in the 1920s and the land used for grazing sheep, until the vineyard was re-established in 1976.
Open: Monday and Wednesday to Friday 09.00–17.00 hrs; Saturday 09.00–18.00 hrs; Sunday 12.00–18.00 hrs; closed Tuesday.
Goonawarra Vineyard, Sunbury Road, Sunbury (tel: 744 1180), dates back to 1858. Its vines were replanted in 1982.
Cellar door open: daily, 09.00–18.00 hrs.
Restaurant: Luncheon, Sunday from noon. Dinner, Wednesday to Saturday from 18.30 hrs. Weekday luncheons are group bookings only.

Victoria's other grape-growing regions include Geelang, Goulburn, Murray Valley, North Eastern and Coonawarra. The booklet *Vintage Victoria— Your Wine and Food Guide* is available from Victour state offices.

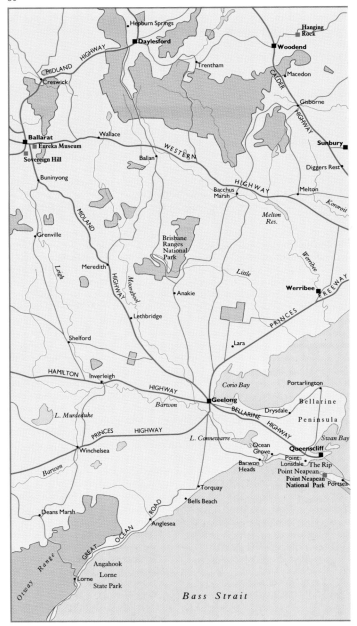

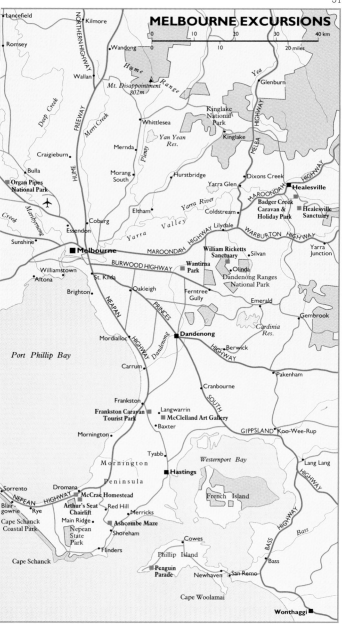

MELBOURNE EXCURSIONS

PEACE AND QUIET

Wildlife and Countryside in Melbourne and Victoria
by Paul Sterry

Melbourne is situated on the shores of Port Phillip Bay and, despite a tendency to sprawl, the city and its surroundings still hold considerable wildlife interest. In addition to parks and gardens within the city boundaries, there are several national parks on Melbourne's outskirts with an attractive cross-section of Victorian habitats. Many of the birds in the city's parks and gardens are accustomed to the presence of man. In addition to native species such as laughing kookaburra, little wattlebird, magpielark and little raven, the introduced starlings and house sparrows can be spotted.

Black swans, often on park lakes

Parkland lakes and ponds often have silver gulls, coots and black swans as well as the occasional Australian pelican or Nankeen night-heron.

To the east of the city lies the Dandenong Ranges National Park. Trails and paths lead through forests of mountain ash and tree ferns which cloak the gullies. The woodlands are home to the superb lyrebirds, whose far-carrying, mimetic songs are a familiar sound throughout the Dandenongs. Mammals are also well-represented: duck-billed platypuses feed in quiet streams, while the forests harbour possums and echidnas.

Kinglake National Park, on the northern outskirts of the city, lies on the Great Dividing Range, and also boasts lush fern gullies. A wealth of plants, including many species of native orchids, such as *Dendrobium* and *Pterostylis*, can be found here, as well as black wallabies and lyrebirds. The nearby Organ Pipes National Park, to the northwest of Melbourne, is also good for wildlife, but is best known for the basalt columns from which its name derives. Also known for its geology, Hanging Rock, near Woodend, can be reached along the Calder Highway.

At the mouth of Port Phillip Bay lies Point Nepean National Park, which protects some of Victoria's finest coastal scenery and harbours colourful bushland flowers in spring. Seabirds such as albatrosses, gulls, shearwaters, cormorants and terns can sometimes be seen offshore and landbirds such as honeyeaters, rainbow bee-eaters and laughing kookaburras add to the variety.

Phillip Island

Phillip Island lies to the south of Melbourne and can be reached via a causeway from the Bass Highway. Although the island has parks and gardens which are good for wildlife and a koala sanctuary which protects Australia's most endearing wildlife symbol, it is for its penguins that it is best known. Summerland Beach, on the west of Phillip Island, has a huge colony of little penguins, sometimes also called little blue or fairy penguins. These engaging birds come ashore at night to visit their nesting burrows and the so-called

Penguin Parade is viewed at this spot with the aid of floodlights. So popular has the spectacle become in recent years that nearly half a million people are estimated to visit the spot each year, especially in summer when the number of penguins swells. Phillip Island is good for many species of seabirds other than the penguins. Pacific gulls, silver gulls and waders such as pied oystercatchers, whimbrels and red-necked stints are found on the shores, while short-tailed shearwaters, which also nest on the island, and albatrosses and Australian gannets stay well offshore.

Port Campbell and Otway National Parks

To the west of Melbourne, on Victoria's south coast, are two national parks which protect the stunning coastal scenery and forests of the Cape Otway region.

Port Campbell National Park, which stretches along the coast from Peterborough in the west almost to Cape Otway itself, has some of the most spectacular coastline to be seen anywhere in the world. Battered relentlessly by the Southern Ocean, sheer cliffs stretch for mile upon mile, leaving eroded archways and limestone stacks including the impressive Twelve Apostles and the Arch.

Offshore islands support breeding seabirds such as short-tailed shearwaters, which may be seen flying on stiff wings out to sea. Lucky visitors may even see southern right whales passing close to land, although 'the coast between

Warrnambool and Port Fairy, further west, is generally considered better.
Otway National Park protects some fine areas of eucalyptus forest, fern gullies and coastal heath which, outside the boundaries of the park, run east to Anglesea. Trails and paths allow easy access to the park and heathland flowers and forest mammals and birds can be superb.

Southwest Victoria
Between Portland and Nelson,

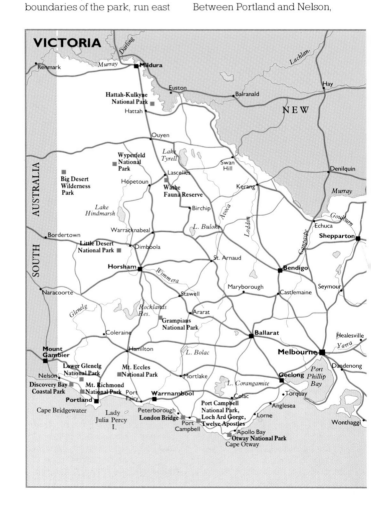

on the state border with South Australia, lies some more wonderfully unspoilt coastline while, inland, three national parks protect volcanic formations, river gorges and forested hills.

The Discovery Bay Coastal Park runs for 30 miles (50km) along the coast from Nelson almost to Cape Bridgewater. The park includes the Great South West Walk, and comprises cliffs, sandy beaches, dunes and marshes. Coastal flowers can be excellent and seabirds such as

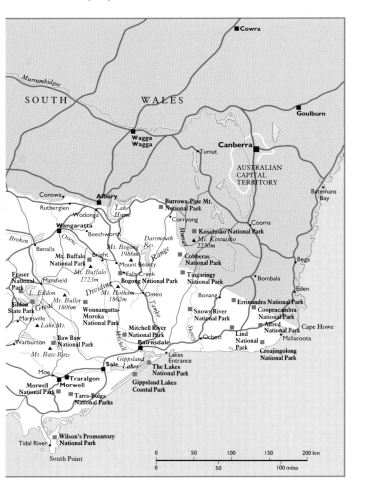

giant petrels, albatrosses, gulls and shearwaters may be seen, depending on the weather conditions and the time of year. Trips can sometimes be arranged from Port Fairy to visit the seabird colonies on Lady Julia Percy Island.

Inland from Nelson, Lower Glenelg National Park encloses forest-clad hills with the River Glenelg's gorge at its heart. Closer to Portland, Mount Eccles and Mount Richmond National Parks harbour long-since extinct volcanoes, as well as volcanic features such as lava flows and craters, which are now lake-filled.

Western Victoria

In the west of Victoria lie two contrasting national parks, one harbouring *mallee* country, the other sandstone outcrops and bush country.

Mallee is the aboriginal name given to a specialised group of gums, which have adapted to dry conditions and have numerous thin trunks arising from a base. This gives them the appearance of coppiced trees. The term is now widely used to describe semi-arid areas cloaked in low scrub and interspersed with areas of heath and sand dune, and Little Desert National Park, to the west of Dimboola, has fine examples of this habitat. Kangaroos and birds such as emu, rainbow bee-eater and malleefowl can be seen, the latter known as 'incubator birds' because of the huge mounds of twigs, leaves and soil in which their eggs are incubated. Decomposition keeps the mound warm and the temperature is carefully monitored and controlled by the male throughout incubation.

Grampians National Park, between Horsham and Hamilton, is Victoria's largest national park. Dominated by sandstone ridges, lakes and waterfalls, Grampians is well known for its scenic beauty and is an excellent site for birds, mammals and colourful flowers.

Wyperfeld National Park

Wyperfeld is an immense national park which lies between Ouyen and Dimboola in the northwest of Victoria, and has over 140,000 acres (100,000 hectares) of *mallee* country. Dry bush habitat and desert sand dunes with scrub cypress pines feature prominently in the landscape, and the wildlife is varied and, not surprisingly, well adapted to the harsh, arid environment. At one time, lake beds periodically filled with water, adding to the variety in habitat and wildlife. Nowadays, due mainly to the increased use of water by the surrounding arable farms, this is a rare occurrence.

Mallee gums are widespread in Wyperfeld, and several species are common. Most impressive of Wyperfeld's marsupial mammals are the kangaroos. Females are sometimes seen accompanied by their young (called 'joeys'), which quickly retreat into the safety of mother's pouch (*marsupium*) at the first sign of danger. In this open country, leaping as a means of locomotion has been perfected by these amazing creatures, who use their powerful hind legs to full

Courting budgies caught stealing a quick peck on the cheek

advantage. Running as a means of escape is also adopted by emus. These huge, flightless birds, as well as kangaroos, are often indifferent to man's presence, and good views can be had.

Like desert areas in many parts of the world, the spring heathland flora can be a riot of colour in Wyperfeld. Bushes of banksias, acacias and cassias, carpets of immortelles and desert species of daisies and orchids are abundant at certain times of year. Butterflies visit the flowers, along with honeyeaters and lorikeets. Rainbow bee-eaters (sometimes called rainbow birds), red-backed kingfishers, superb blue fairywrens, crested pigeons and budgerigars all add to the wealth of wildlife.

Hattah-Kulkyne National Park

The mighty Murray River marks the northern boundary of Victoria with New South Wales.

PEACE AND QUIET

The red kangaroo is a force to be reckoned with when it shakes a leg

The river has a profound effect on the surrounding countryside, feeding the farmlands of the Murray Valley and creating lakes and wetlands which are havens to wildlife. One of the most interesting areas in the region is the Hattah-Kulkyne National Park near Mildura in northwest Victoria: the Hattah Lakes are periodically flooded by the river and host wetland species of birds. The supply of water also acts as a magnet for the creatures of the dry, *mallee* bush country, which is the dominant habitat in the park. As well as being a state border, the Murray River also serves as the eastern boundary of the national park. The river banks are lined with immense red gums, which are the haunt of mulga parrots, regent parrots, sulphur crested cockatoos, pink cockatoos, galahs, lorikeets and rosellas, and under which camping is permitted in certain areas. Many species nest in the

security of holes in the trees, but still have to keep a sharp look-out for predatory monitor lizards. Among the marsupial mammals of Hattah-Kulkyne are several species of kangaroo and wallaby, including Australia's most impressive animal, the red kangaroo. When standing tall on their hind legs, these kangaroos are taller than a man and can maintain a steady 30mph (48kph) hop for considerable distances. Many of the park's other mammals are nocturnal, but visitors should have no problem seeing emus, laughing kookaburras and malleefowl (or at least their mounds). When water conditions in the park's lakes are right, the bird life often becomes concentrated. The numbers of wildfowl such as black swans, musk ducks, chestnut teals, pink-eared ducks, white-eyed ducks and

Australian wood ducks are unpredictable, but they can be common. Wading in the shallow margins of the lakes in search of fish and amphibians are white-necked herons, straw-necked ibises, white ibises, little egrets and spoonbills.

Mount Buffalo National Park

Mount Buffalo National Park lies between Wangaratta and Bright, in northeast Victoria, and offers some of the most magnificent alpine scenery to be found in the state. From the lookout on Mount Buffalo's plateau, the views are panoramic, with snow-capped peaks towering above forests in the valley of the Ovens River below. Elsewhere in the park, waterfalls, such as the Eurobin Falls, and cliffs are spectacular. The snows of the Victorian Alps, which blanket the higher slopes and lure many visitors to Mount Buffalo National Park for the winter sports, also serve to insulate the ground flora from the worst excesses of temperature. Come spring, when the temperature rises and the snow melts, carpets of alpine flowers, such as mountain gentians, alpine mint bush, mountain milkwort and orchids, burst into life.

Northeast Victoria

Close to the border with New South Wales, the terrain becomes wild and remote. Fortunately, many of the best areas are now protected within the boundaries of national parks and the scenery and habitat is remarkably varied: Bogong National Park boasts dramatic alpine scenery, while Errinundra has temperate rainforests.

The vivid colours of a crimson rosella can sometimes be spotted

Elsewhere, river valleys, cliffs, plateaux, waterfalls and forests all add to the diversity of the region.

Bogong National Park is situated near the town of Mount Beauty, to the east of Mount Buffalo National Park. Dominated by Mount Bogong, Mount Feathertop and Mount Hotham, the park holds Victoria's highest peaks, and winter sports are popular here.

Above the treeline, various colourful alpine flowers such as mountain gentians, alpine groundsels and silvery daisies can be found in profusion in spring, while, at lower altitudes, forests of snow gums are a feature of the landscape and harbour wedgetail eagles, rosellas and cockatoos, which nest in the ancient trees.

While its peaks lack the grand scale of those in Bogong,

PEACE AND QUIET

Burrowa-Pine Mountain National Park, on the border with New South Wales, near Corryong, has some impressive scenery, with waterfalls and dramatic outcrops of rock. To the south, Cobberas and Tingaringy National Parks also have mountains with forested slopes and rushing torrents, and trails through both parks allow extensive exploration.

Snowy River National Park is one of Victoria's largest and most spectacular parks. The Snowy River, after which the park is named, has carved deep gorges in places, and the more gentle valley slopes are now cloaked in dense forest. The nearby Errinundra National Park, to the east of the Bonang Highway, is also heavily wooded and has some fine areas of temperate rainforest, an unusual and declining habitat.

Just over the border into New South Wales lies the Kosciusko National Park, which contains Australia's highest mountains.

A well-named scarlet robin

Forests of snow gum and mountain ash cloak the lower slopes, while, above the treeline, alpine meadows host a profusion of spring flowers.

Croajingolong National Park

For lovers of coastal scenery, Croajingolong National Park, in the east of Victoria, is not to be missed. The park runs from the New South Wales border west for over 60 miles (100km), and boasts mile after mile of deserted beach, as well as mudflats, cliffs, headlands, coastal heaths and forests. Croajingolong is popular with Victoria's visitors and residents alike, but because much of it can only be explored on foot, peace and quiet can be guaranteed away from the main centres. Many visitors make the settlement at Mallacoota their base, from where the beautiful Mallacoota Inlet can be explored by boat. Dense forests, ringing to the calls and songs of birds, grow almost down to the water's edge, and provide a wonderful backdrop for a cruise. Almost any place along the coast will provide stunning scenery and a rich variety of wildlife. Windswept cliff-tops are often cloaked in coastal heath vegetation which bursts into flower in spring. Birds such as honeyeaters and thornbills feed among the vegetation and flowers, while kookaburras perch and scan the ground for lizards and insects. Headlands and promontories provide visitors with a chance to see, albeit at a distance, a variety of seabirds flying by, such as shearwaters, cormorants, giant petrels and perhaps albatrosses. Beaches anywhere are likely to be frequented by silver gulls and Pacific gulls, while migrant waders, including whimbrels, bar-tailed godwits and red-necked stints, do not tolerate disturbance and prefer secluded shores.

Away from the coast, the forests are home to secretive mammals, colourful butterflies and lots of birds. Blossom-feeding species, such as rainbow lorikeets and honeyeaters, flock to flowering trees and bushes, but many other woodland species such as flame robins and scarlet robins are much less conspicuous. Further inland, Lind and Alfred National Parks protect tiny remnants of temperate rainforest, harbouring birds such as crimson rosellas, while Coopracambra National Park, on the New South Wales border, combines challenging walking country with rugged, eroded sandstone scenery.

Fraser National Park, Eildon State Park and Wonnangatta-Moroka National Park

Fraser National Park and nearby Eildon State Park both lie on the shores of Lake Eildon, a man-made reservoir less than 100 miles (160km) from Melbourne. The lake is popular with watersports enthusiasts and wildfowl, and provides a beautiful setting for the rolling hills of the parks.

The typical vegetation around Lake Eildon is grassland dotted with gum trees. Birds such as rosellas, cockatoos, laughing kookaburras, Australian magpies and rainbow bee-eaters, and mammals such as wombats can be seen; but it is the grey kangaroos for which Fraser National Park in particular is best known. These huge animals are generally almost indifferent to the presence of man and often can be watched at close quarters if treated with a degree of respect.

Wonnangatta-Moroka National Park lies further east, on the Great Dividing Range. As you might expect, the scenery is impressive with dramatic cliffs and gorges and large areas of the park can be explored on foot or by ski.

The Morwell Area

Morwell lies 93 miles (150km) to the east of Melbourne along the Princes Highway. It is a centre from which the visitor can explore three small, but nevertheless interesting, national parks, each with its own unique character.

Baw Baw National Park, to the north of Morwell, is the largest of the three and is dominated by the rugged appearance of the weathered granite plateau. A network of paths makes backpacking a popular pursuit in summer, but the long-distance trail from Walhalla to Warburton should only be undertaken by experienced walkers. In winter the park's appearance is very different, when cross-country skiing replaces hiking as the best way to explore Baw Baw.

Morwell National Park, south of Morwell on Midland Highway, is tiny by comparison with Baw Baw, but has a distinctly luxuriant appearance. The

PEACE AND QUIET

dense forests, which cloak the steep slope of the Strzelecki Ranges, have a rich understorey of ferns and are home to a variety of mammals and birds such as lyrebirds, scarlet robins and white-browed scrubwrens. However, for really impressive stands of ferns, the Tarra Valley and adjacent Bulga National Parks should be visited.

Tarra Valley and Bulga are small, isolated remnants of the magnificent rainforest that once cloaked the hills of southern Victoria. Much of the surrounding land has long since been cleared and no longer supports the national parks' mountain ash, blackwood and tree ferns. Gone as well from most of the surrounding land are the forest mammals such as wallabies, sugar gliders, duck-billed platypuses and echidnas, as well as birds such as whipbirds, rosellas and superb lyrebirds. However, the forested valleys of Tarra and Bulga still ring to the wonderful songs and calls of this latter species, which is justly famous for its amazing ability to mimic the songs of its fellow forest inhabitants.

Forest trails and nature walks help guide visitors to the best spots and minimise the environmental impact of trampling feet. For the moment, this approach seems to be working, and a rich carpet of ferns and orchids such as greenhoods and maroonhoods greets the eye. Away from ground level, the humidity and rainfall allow epiphytic plants to grow in profusion, including species of *Dendrobium*.

The delicate greenhood orchid thrives in the forests of Tarra Valley and Bulga

The Bairnsdale Area

Bairnsdale is situated on the Mitchell River, close to Lake King. This huge body of water, together with Lakes Wellington and Victoria, comprises the Gippsland Lakes and forms one of the largest inland water body complexes in Australia. The lakes are only just inland, however, being separated from the sea by a long spit of land, Ninety Mile Beach, itself dissected by Lake Reeve.

At its southwestern end, the area is protected by the Gippsland Lakes Coastal Park, near Sale, while further along the spit at Sperm Whale Head, the Lakes National Park has its headquarters. Not surprisingly, resident and migrant waterbirds and seabirds are a highlight of the area, but the national park's kangaroos should not be missed. Follow the course of the Mitchell River inland from Bairnsdale and you will eventually come to the Mitchell River National Park at Glenaladale. Trails, paths and canoes help visitors explore this splendid area of rainforest, which is home to parrots, lyrebirds, wallabies and echidnas.

Wilson's Promontory National Park

Wilson's Promontory, which has been a national park since the turn of the century, is a rocky outcrop lying at the end of a narrow and low-lying strip of land, 124 miles (200km) southeast of Melbourne. Surrounded by the waters of the Bass Strait on three sides, the area's separation from mainland Victoria has given it a degree of isolation that is not shared by the state's other coastal parks. A single road leads on to Wilson's Promontory and terminates at Tidal River. Thereafter, exploration must continue on foot, but the effort required is soon rewarded.

For lovers of the outdoors, Wilson's Promontory National Park has got everything. In addition to the superb coastal scenery, which comprises wonderful beaches and cliffs, there are immense outcrops of granite, coastal heathland, rainforests and fern gullies. This is one of the state's most popular and attractive national parks. A network of trails of varying length enable visitors of almost any experience and interest to explore Wilson's Promontory to the full. For those wishing more than a day's visit, lodges and campsites permit a lengthy stay. From coastal walks, shorebirds and seabirds can be seen, while, on land, spring flowers on the heaths, such as banksias, bottlebrushes and Victorian heath, attract a variety of insects and birds.

Over the last century, the ravages of fire and tree-felling have, unfortunately, impoverished the woodlands and forest wildlife of the national park's interior, although areas of gum forest and rainforest still persist. Gullies full of ferns and epiphytes testify to the richness of the natural environment which, were it not for the impact of man, would be far more widespread than it is now. In today's more open woodland, however, those creatures that remain are often easier to see.

FOOD AND DRINK

FOOD AND DRINK

Eating Out

It is said that you can eat your way around the world without leaving Melbourne, and with over 2,000 restaurants, this is arguably Australia's culinary capital. Restaurants are either licensed or BYO—which means Bring Your Own wine or beer, reducing the cost of your meal. Australian meals were rather basic for a long time. There was nearly always the Sunday roast, beef or lamb and three vegetables—potatoes, pumpkin and beans or peas: nothing very imaginative. All that changed when the first wave of Europeans started arriving after World War II. They could not find the foods to which they were accustomed, so they opened cafés and shops to cater for their needs. When

BYO – Bring Your Own – is a cost-cutting option at meal times

Asians came in great numbers in more recent years, they did the same. There are now ethnic cafés serving foods of nearly every nationality. Many are run by families, using family recipes just as mother used to make—and sometimes it is actually mother who is cooking. Certain streets are noted for a particular cuisine—Chinese in Little Bourke Street, City (Chinatown); Greek in Swan Street, Richmond; Italian in Lygon Street, Carlton; Vietnamese in Victoria Street, Abbotsford. Brunswick Street, Fitzroy, has the greatest variety of ethnic restaurants. The cafés stand side by side with the more up-market, more professional restaurants, where chefs are local or brought in from Europe or Asia. Good restaurants are located all over Melbourne and the suburbs, not just in the centre of the city, and it has become popular with Melburnians to travel out of town. See **Accommodation**, page 79, for top-class hotel restaurants.

If you are touring around Victoria many country towns have both small cafés serving home-made snacks and more sophisticated restaurants specialising in country cooking.

As elsewhere in the world there is a trend towards health foods, home-made and hand-made foods: bread baked in wood-fired ovens, organic fruit and vegetables, fresh pasta are all widely available.

Because of the varying climatic zones in Australia most fruits and vegetables can be grown there. As tastes have widened, so the demand for more unusual varieties are grown, from tropical fruits to herbs. Occasionally you see some imported fruits, such as grapefruit from California, and there is an enormous amount of food imported from Europe and Asia, though local products are improving all the time. Cheese and butter from King Island, off the coast of Tasmania, is being compared with the best of French. If you see that name try some.

Australians have long had the reputation as great beer drinkers, and there is a wide choice of local or imported brands. But Melburnians today have also become critical connoisseurs of wine. Locally grown wine is becoming better and better and internationally acclaimed; mineral water, too, is popular. Look out for local brands, particularly from the natural springs at Hepburn Springs.

It is difficult to pinpoint foods which are identified with Australia, but among the items claimed as their own by Australians are: Vegemite, pavlova (the meringue dessert also claimed by New Zealanders), lamingtons (small, square sponges covered with chocolate and coconut), and damper (unyeasted bread, traditionally made in the bush).

Top-class Restaurants

Many of the top restaurants in Melbourne are based on traditional French cuisine, with their own individual touches, and are often expensive. Here are a few of the many.

Cafe Florentino, 80 Bourke Street, City (tel: 662 1811), recently changed owners. It has been renovated, but retained touches of the old style. It remains a top restaurant with Italian cuisine.

Fanny's, 243 Lonsdale Street, City (tel: 663 3017), is another Melbourne 'institution', owned by the same family for more than 30 years. The *doyenne*, Gloria Staley, still devises the menus. There is a bistro downstairs which serves simpler and cheaper dishes.

Maxim's, 632 Chapel Street, South Yarra (tel: 266 5500), has nothing to do with Maxim's of Paris. It is, however, similarly exclusive, and atmospheric. For 32 years it was situated in the centre of the South Yarra shopping area, and has recently

FOOD AND DRINK

moved to a lavish, modern venue within the new Como project, complete with its famous mural of old Paris and the delightful owner, Vincent Rosales, who greets every customer as a friend.

Maxim's has long been *the* restaurant for special celebrations. Traditionally the owner of the Melbourne Cup winner has celebrated at Maxim's after the horse race and it has the most exclusive take-away service: a complete dinner can be delivered to your home, and each guest room at the luxurious Hotel Como has a direct line to Maxim's for room service!

Mietta's, 7 Alfred Place, off either Collins or Little Collins Street between Russell and Exhibition Streets (tel: 654 2366). There is no other restaurant in Melbourne, or Australia, like Mietta's. It has a true Victorian

atmosphere including a Parisian-style salon, and the building itself dates back to 1886. It has had an illustrious background, originally the German Club, and then for more than 50 years the Naval and Military Club. Mietta's bought it in 1984 and restored it. It is tucked away in a laneway, away from the bustle of the city streets, and once inside, you step back into the grandeur and elegance of a bygone era. A beautiful staircase sweeps up to the restaurant, the former ballroom, full of antique furniture and silver, flowers and candelabra which glow with candlelight at night. Mietta and her partner Tony Knox are following on with the restaurant tradition of her grandparents who opened one of the great Italian restaurants in Melbourne

Experience the glittering opulence of the Victorian age in Mietta's

in the 1940s. It is noted for its Burgundy wines which are imported direct from the vineyards in France. Downstairs is The Lounge, a bistro and bar, open from 11.00–03.00 hrs every day—a grand meeting place for coffee, champagne and after-theatre suppers, with armchairs and sofas alongside small tables and chairs. On Sundays it becomes an informal salon with varied forms of entertainment—writers or poets read their works, an Opera star sings, there might be a jazz concert or a recital by a pianist. Open daily.

Le Restaurant in the **Regent Hotel** (see page 81) has the best view of Melbourne: a magical place for dinner at night.

Stephanie's, 405 Tooronga Road, Hawthorn (tel: 822 8944), is a complete dining experience, acclaimed as the finest restaurant in Australia. Owner/chef Stephanie Alexander is renowned for her imaginative use of ingredients and the adventurous touches to classic French cuisine, and her restaurant is set in a beautiful Victorian terrace house.

Nothing could be grander than dining in The Grand Dining Room of the old **Windsor Hotel** (see page 82). All the traditional luxury of a bygone age is here—domed ceiling, chandeliers and orchestral trio. One of the menus specialises in game, and the Windsor Lounge, with its leather seating, is *the* place for morning or afternoon tea.

Other top restaurants, not quite as expensive, include:

The Society, 23 Bourke Street, City (tel: 654 5378), is one of the oldest Italian restaurants in Melbourne. The menu is small and specialised with an Italian flavour.

Chinois, 176 Toorak Road, South Yarra (tel: 826 3388), a fascinating blend of flavours, superb presentation and exquisite décor, with black-rimmed, white plates with black chopsticks or cutlery. There is a bar, upstairs and downstairs restaurants. Open daily, for lunch, dinner and snacks. See also **Marchetti's Latin**, page 68.

Ethnic

There are an endless number of restaurants which specialise in a particular type of cuisine, mainly Chinese, Vietnamese, Greek and Italian. They can be up-market and expensive or small and very cheap; simply or ornately furnished. The smaller restaurants sometimes do not take credit cards. Some have become so popular, the owners have opened a second restaurant.

Chinese: Chinese cuisine is centred around Chinatown, Little Bourke Street, but there are Chinese cafés everywhere, in suburbs and country towns.

The Flower Drum, 17 Market Lane, off Little Bourke Street, City (tel: 662 3655), has long had the reputation of being the best Chinese (Cantonese) restaurant in Melbourne. Lunch Monday to Friday only; dinner nightly. Expensive.

King Wah, 233 Lonsdale Street, City (tel: 663 1844), was one of the first Chinese restaurants in Melbourne to serve *yum cha*,

FOOD AND DRINK

and is still popular for its trolley service.

Supper Inn, 15–17 Celestial Avenue, off Little Bourke Street (tel: 663 4759), as its name implies, is especially noted for its suppers, and stays open until about 02.00 hrs. Inexpensive.

French: For a real touch of France, the bistro **France-Soir**, 11 Toorak Road, South Yarra (tel: 266 8569), has French chefs, waiters and lots of French customers. The tables covered with white butcher's paper, delicious casseroles made from home recipes.

Greek: Swan Street, Richmond, is full of Greek cafés, with a few in *Little Greece*, part of Lonsdale Street. **Laikon**, 272 Swan Street, Richmond (tel: 428 6983), has no menu: you choose your own food from the counter. **Kaliva Restaurant**, 256 Swan Street, Richmond (tel: 428 7028), has live music to accompany your meal. **The Greek Deli**, 583 Chapel Street, South Yarra (tel: 241 3734), is worth a visit; the whole trout charcoal-grilled is great.

Indian: Nawab's, 312 Brunswick Street, Fitzroy (tel: 419 0861), is reputed to have the best Indian food in Melbourne. Moderate. **The Tandoor**, 517 Chapel Street, South Yarra (tel: 241 8247), has cool and understated décor with a wide choice of individual dishes and suggested menus. Moderate.

Italian: Lygon Street, Carlton, is Italy in Melbourne. It is full of Italian cafés, coffee places, pizza and gelati parlours, all with a friendly atmosphere which only an Italian café can have.

Amaretto, 205 Victoria Parade,

Fitzroy (tel: 417 5169). The ultimate in Italian friendliness.

Caffe e Cucina, 581 Chapel Street, South Yarra (tel: 241 4139), is a little café with a big following. Popular for breakfast—freshly squeezed orange juice, pips and all, focaccia with ham and cheese, and wonderful coffee served in glass.

Campari, 25 Hardware Street, City (tel: 670 3813), is a popular place, with Italian-style salads attractively displayed all day. Granita, lemon over crushed ice is refreshing. Inexpensive.

Donnini's, 312 Drummond Street, Carlton (tel: 347 3128), was one of the first Italian restaurants to serve home-made pasta. Moderate. They have a shop around the corner, also **Donnini's**, 389 Lygon Street (tel: 347 1655), where you can buy their pasta and sauces.

Gepetto, 78a Wellington Parade, East Melbourne (tel: 417 4691). A quiet café, in a quiet area, inexpensive, and **La Camera**, 446 Chapel Street, South Yarra (tel: 241 8531), with good home-style cooking.

La Rustica, 287 Victoria Street, West Melbourne (tel: 328 3013). A wide range of dishes such as hearty beef and veal casseroles. On Monday to Wednesday evenings as much pasta as you can eat for a fixed price.

Others include **Marchetti's Latin**, 55 Lonsdale Street, City (tel: 662 1985), one of the top restaurants in Melbourne, and a grand old-style Italian restaurant. Expensive.

Maria's Trattoria, 122 Peel Street, North Melbourne (tel: 329 9016), is a simple café with a great

Good food at a top hotel: the Regent

reputation for home-made food: a favourite with university professors as well as students. Near the Queen Victoria Market. Inexpensive.

Topo Gigio, 432 Toorak Road, Toorak (tel: 241 5555), serves a whole range of good, simple Italian dishes.

Waiter's Restaurant, 20 Meyers Place, City (tel: 650 1508), is a Melbourne institution—starting out as an eating place for Italian waiters after they had finished work at the nearby hotels and restaurants. When people other than waiters began to go its popularity grew, but it is still hard to find as the name is only inside. It is in a laneway behind the Windsor Hotel, and has a number 20 on a door—go up the steep wooden steps, open the door and you are there.

Pizzas: Papa Gino's, 221 Lygon Street, Carlton (tel: 347 5758), has pizzas which melt in your mouth. At **Da Salvatore**, 132 Lygon Street, Carlton (tel: 663 4778), you can buy pizza by the metre.

Japanese: There are now more than 60 Japanese restaurants in Melbourne. **Kuni's**, 27 Crossley Lane, City (tel: 663 7243), was the first to introduce a *sushi* bar to Melbourne. **Kenzan**, Collins Place, 45 Collins Street, lower ground floor (tel: 654 8933), is very elegant with waitresses in kimonos. *Sushi* and *sashami* are available at the *sushi* bar or tables.

Lebanese: Mount Lebanon, 177 Toorak Road, South Yarra (tel: 240 9080), has plush red curtains and comfortable banquettes and a set menu or choice of individual dishes. Live music and belly dancers often encourage customers to join in.

FOOD AND DRINK

Abla's, 109 Elgin Street, Carlton (tel: 347 0006), is noted for its authentic home cooking.
Malaysian: Penang Affair, 325 Brunswick Street, Fitzroy (tel: 417 7584), was so popular the owner has opened a second restaurant, **Penang Lily**, 263 Brunswick Street, Fitzroy (tel: 417 6940), with similar food, but Lily is more Thai.
Malaysian Delight, 1335 Burke Road, East Kew (tel: 817 2459), is delightful and cheap.
Turkish: Sydney Road, Brunswick, is noted for its Turkish restaurants and comes alive at night with flashing neon signs outside the restaurants. Some have seating for up to two hundred, and cater for families, friends and children, and always have a friendly atmosphere. **The Turkish Palace**, 831 Sydney Road, Brunswick (tel: 386 3462). If you are keen on brains and sweetbreads and other delicate parts of the anatomy, they are at their best here, and the tripe soup, and the salads specialities are great too.
Zara's, 169 Sydney Road, Coburg (tel: 384 1415), is a very welcoming restaurant, with a bakery at one end where you can see beautiful, large, flat loaves of bread being baked in the wood oven. Eat it still warm, and so fresh that it melts in your mouth.
Adana, 848 Sydney Road, Brunswick (tel: 386 2608). The bread is freshly baked here, too, and is excellent with the dips.

Turkish restaurants are one ingredient in Melbourne's rich cultural mix

Alasya 2, 163 Sydney Road, Brunswick (tel: 387 6914), has a sister restaurant further up the road: **Alasya**, 555 Sydney Road, Brunswick (tel: 387 2679); both are very popular.

Vietnamese is the newest cuisine to come to Melbourne, centred on Victoria Street, Richmond.

Thy Thy, first floor, 142 Victoria Street, Richmond (tel: 429 1104), is very good, very simple and very cheap, while **Thy Thy**, first floor, 116 Victoria Street, Richmond (tel: 428 5914), is slightly more up-market, but still good and simple. Both can get very crowded, and remember that Vietnamese tend to eat earlier at night.

Que Huong, 176 Bridge Road, Richmond (tel: 429 1213), is highly decorated and serves excellent food.

Seafood
Jean Jacques by the Sea, 40 Jacka Boulevard, St Kilda (tel: 534 8221), as its name suggests, is right on the beach with an uninterrupted view of Port Phillip Bay; a wonderful setting for a seafood restaurant, the most exclusive in Melbourne. Very expensive. There is, however, a take-away section which you can enjoy—perhaps on the beach! **The Last Aussie Fishcaf**, 256 Park Street, South Melbourne (tel: 699 1942), is a fun fish café, with décor and sounds from the '50s, from a juke box, and rock 'n' roll dancing.

Steak
Vlado's Charcoal Grill, 61 Bridge Road, Richmond (tel: 428 5833), is noted for its steak, the best in Melbourne. You choose your cut,

Seafood – a shore certainty

and it is grilled to your liking, with Vlado's special sausages. Open for lunch, Monday to Friday; dinner, Monday to Saturday. Closed Sundays. Bookings essential.

Vegetarian
Shakahari, 329 Lygon Street, Carlton (tel: 347 3848), is the best vegetarian: tasty, original and with an Asian touch.

International
Some more interesting places to try include:
African Tukul Eating House, 517 Chapel Street, South Yarra (tel: 241 8247). Many new dishes introduced via the owner's African customers, with an emphasis on beans.
Café Lisboa, 413 Brunswick Street, Fitzroy (tel: 419 9103). Everything is Portuguese here from the dishes to the wines, and

FOOD AND DRINK

even the mineral water.
Californian-style at Brophy's, 34 Jackson Street, Toorak (tel: 241 3266). A contemporary restaurant with bar and lovely balcony setting for summer, serving luncheons and dinners. Expensive.
Jamaica House, 106 Lygon Street, Carlton (tel: 663 5715). Curry and spicy dishes. Moderate.
Mexicali Rose, 103 Swan Street, Richmond (tel: 42 9555). Authentic Mexican dishes.
Punjab, 450 Bridge Road, Richmond (tel: 428 8699), is a Pakistani café with a wide range of dishes. Inexpensive.

Where to drink

Pubs
The old-style Australian hotel has been given a new lease of life in recent years and pubs and hotels remain the most popular places to drink. Modern-style restaurants, bistros and bars have been incorporated within many an elderly frame.
The Lemon Tree Hotel, 10 Grattan Street, Carlton (tel: 347 7514), set the trend, bars and restaurants in different settings. The adjoining **Alphington House**, 2 Grattan Street, Carlton (tel: 347 1510), has a sophisticated pub atmosphere within a restored terrace house. You can sit informally at a bar or at tables with beer or wine and champagne and eat imaginative snacks.
Lord Newry Hotel, 543 Brunswick Street, North Fitzroy (tel: 481 3931), has changed little over the last hundred years from the outside, but its interior has been tastefully modernised. There is a street bar called Toby's Bar and a bar upstairs called Upstairs at the Newry and a restaurant, Mostly French. The menu includes charcoal-grilled sardines or octopus, and lambs' fry served with crispy bacon and onion rings on toast.
Fawkner Club Hotel, 52 Toorak Road, South Yarra (tel: 266 1679), features a beer garden, especially popular with the younger generation. There live jazz is performed on Sunday.

Good cocktails make good neighbours

SHOPPING

Melbourne has every type of shop imaginable, from department stores to specialised shops to markets.

As well as the large shopping centres of the outer suburbs, there are streets which are particularly noted for their shops: Toorak Road for exclusive fashion boutiques, Chapel Street for young fashions, and High Street, Armadale, for antiques. Australia's first Japanese department store, Daimaru, is scheduled to open in Melbourne at the end of 1991. Daily shopping expeditions are offered by **Rosalind's Shopping Tours** (tel: 267 1355) and **Jackie's Tours** (tel: 347 5655).

Discount shopping trips to Melbourne's factory outlets are offered by **Pamm's Shopping Tours** (tel: 592 6911) and **Shopping Spree Tours** (tel: 543 5855).

There are a number of shops in the city centre where you can purchase a range of goods duty-free if you hold an international flight ticket (departing from Melbourne Airport). The most central is **City International Duty Free**, 184/206 Swanston Street, (tel: 650 3258). There are also duty-free shops at the airport.

Australiana

Aboriginal Handicrafts, ninth floor, Century Building, 125–133 Swanston Street, City (tel: 650 4717). Boomerangs, music sticks, bark paintings and woven bags hand-crafted by Aborigines.

Antipodes, 22 Toorak Road, South Yarra (tel: 266 5749). A very good selection of high-quality goods.

Australiana General Store, 1227 High Street, Armadale (tel: 822 2324), has gifts for everybody, from babies to business executives.

Woodworks, 308 Chapel Street, specialises in wooden articles, many from Australian timbers. Award-winning designer **Moira Wallis** has some wonderful gifts made from natural fabrics, including the 'Pollution Solution' bag, cotton and washable. For details of shop outlets, tel: 654 4525.

Books

Books are not hard to come by in Melbourne, whether in the chain and discount bookshops of the city, or the more specialised boutiques in the suburbs. **Angus and Robertson**, 107 Elizabeth Street, City, and **Collins**, 117 Elizabeth Street, City, are the two best-known chains, with city stores almost next to each other. Some smaller shops have recently introduced comfortable seating, a background of classical music, live jazz, readings and personal appearances by writers, which all go to create a more intimate atmosphere.

There are lounge chairs in the **Brunswick Street Book Shop**, 311 Brunswick Street, Fitzroy (tel: 416 1030), and **Hartwig's Books**, 245 Brunswick Street, Fitzroy (tel: 417 7147). **The Black Mask**, 78 Toorak Road, South Yarra (tel: 267 2717), has assistants who are expert and friendly. **Cosmos** is at 112 Ackland Street, St Kilda (tel: 534 4568), and at 269 Swanston Street, City (tel: 663 1621). **The ABC (Australian**

SHOPPING

Browsers and people-watchers gather at Queen Victoria Market

Broadcasting Corporation) Bookshop, State Bank Centre, 385 Bourke Street, City, has a great range of books and videos from many of their television series.
The Arts Bookshop, 1067 High Street, Armadale (tel: 20 2645), specialises in new and second-hand books on the visual arts. For lovers of antiquarian books, **Kay Craddock**, Cavendish House, corner of Flinders Lane and Russell Street (tel: 654 8506 and 654 7530), are specialists in Australiana, the Pacific and Indian Ocean region, Antarctica and Asia. **Gaston Renard**, 51 Sackville Street, corner of Wellington Street, Collingwood (tel: 417 1944), is another place to try, and **Peter Arnold**, 463 High Street, Prahran (tel: 529 2933), has fine and rare books on Australiana.

Crafts
The Little Gallery, 3 Village Walk, 493 Toorak Road, Toorak (tel: 241 0504). Hand-crafted glass, pottery and paintings by local crafts people.
Makers Mark, 85 Collins Street, City (tel: 654 8488). A superb collection of beautifully hand-crafted jewellery and other items by leading Australian gold and silversmiths. Some pieces

feature Australian flora and fauna.

Fashions
Morrisons Australia, 462 Chapel Street, South Yarra (tel: 241 8255). Up-market Australian country-style clothes, including lambskin jackets.
RM Williams, Shop 3, State Bank Galleria, Elizabeth Street, City (tel: 670 7400). Original bushman's outfitters, which have become fashionable for city, as well as country, men and women. Moleskins, boots, oilskin coats and Akubra hats.

Florists
The best flowers in Melbourne are from **Kevin O'Neill**, 119 Toorak Road, South Yarra (tel: 266 5776). He is known throughout Australia, and has travelled overseas to select and arrange flowers for receptions. If you want a pot plant or shrub as a gift, there is a lovely range at **Jenny Walker's Nursery** at 573–577 High Street, East Prahran (tel: 51 4850).

Gems
You can buy Australian opals at sales tax free prices if you produce your passport and flight ticket. Make sure you only buy from reputable dealers; ask at the **Victour** office.
Gemtec, seventh floor, 124 Exhibition Street, City (tel: 654 5733), sells loose opals, which can be good for investment, or individually designed jewellery featuring opals.
You can watch opals being cut at **Andrew Cody**, first floor, 119 Swanston Street, City (tel: 654 5533). **The Opal Mine**, Shoppers'

Paradise, 127 Bourke Street (tel: 650 3566), sells loose opals and produces jewellery to order.

Markets
Melburnians love to shop at markets. The produce can be fresher and cheaper, and the variety greater than in shops; but many go just to enjoy the unique bustling, the friendly atmosphere. Of the many food markets in the suburbs, these are the best known:
Prahran Market, 177 Commercial Road, Prahran (tel: 522 3302). Beautifully displayed fruit and vegetables, and a huddle of shops attached to the market, overflowing with different cheeses, bags of nuts and gleaming tins of black olives. There is a courtyard to sit and have a cup of coffee and listen to the street musicians (open: Tuesday and Thursday 07.30–17.00 hrs; Friday 06.00–18.00 hrs; Saturday 06.00–13.00 hrs). Tram 6 from Swanston Street.
Queen Victoria Market, corner of Elizabeth and Victoria Streets (tel: 658 9600), is Melbourne's biggest and most exciting market of all. There has been a market on this site since 1859, and some of the old buildings have been restored. Over a thousand stalls sell an enormous variety of foods, clothing and bric-à-brac. Row after row of fruits and vegetables, cheese and salami and sausages. Whatever you want can be bought in this clean and colourful market, and you can stand and tuck in to a capuccino, roll and bratwurst sausage or other snacks.

SHOPPING

Fruit and vegetables are not sold on Sundays, which are best for clothes, shoes, materials and jewellery (open: Tuesday and Thursday 06.00–14.00 hrs; Saturday 06.00–12.00 hrs; Sunday 09.00–16.00 hrs). Tram (any number) in Elizabeth Street northbound to stop 12.

South Melbourne Market, corner of Coventry and Cecil Streets, South Melbourne (tel: 695 8294). This is a small, intimate market for food and clothing, much favoured by local people (open: Wednesday 07.30–14.00 hrs; Friday 07.30–18.00 hrs; Saturday 07.30–12.30 hrs; Sunday 07.30–16.00 hrs).

Malls, Arcades and Department Stores

Melbourne is known for its glass-lit arcades and fine stores—some of the best in Australia. In the centre of the city, buskers, mime artists and office workers join the crowds of shoppers in Bourke Street's mall, between Swanston Street and Elizabeth Street.

Spread over two buildings in Bourke and Lonsdale Streets and connected by a raised walkway, is **Myer**, established in 1914 and said to be the largest department store in the southern hemisphere. You can buy just about anything at Myer, including the proverbial kitchen sink. In the fashion department, a consultant can help you choose and advise you on the clothes to buy, selecting items from different departments for you to view. There is a good book department, with an excellent selection of Australian titles; and, for gift-hunters, a range of

Australian souvenirs. You can buy groceries, a gourmet sandwich or choose from many types of bread, including a damper, the unyeasted bread that was traditionally made in the bush in an open fire. There is a pleasant and quiet restaurant on the sixth floor, Bourke Street. And at Christmas the windows fronting the mall are alive with wonderful clockwork tableaux.

David Jones, a prominent Sydney company, opened its shop in Melbourne a few years ago. It has a similar but smaller range of products as Myer, in three stores, and offers a delivery service to hotels (tel: 669 8200). The store in Little Lonsdale Street houses beautiful accessories for the home, and on the opposite side of the mall, the newer store's main attraction is the Food Hall, 'Food Glorious Food', complete with suggested menus and recipes, including the shopping list of ingredients available from the different counters, and advice on the accompanying wines (which, of course, you can also buy there!).

Fronting the mall is the lovely old **Royal Arcade**. Dating back to the 1860s, the arcade's façade has a corrugated iron roof above the pavement, supported by slim pillars. Delicate iron arches and scrolls decorate the interior, which has a glass roof and black and white tiled floor. At the far wall is a clock featuring the mythical giant figures of Gog and Magog, who have been striking the clock at quarter-hour intervals since 1892. Old Father Time holds an hour glass above

Even the choosiest shoppers should find what they want at Myer

the entrance to the arcade, which goes through to Little Collins Street.

If you walk down a few stairs within the arcade, you will come to **Quist's**, a very special coffee shop, in a little offshoot of an arcade called The Hub. The coffee is served in a large glass cup and is very, very good. There are complimentary cookies for you to serve yourself at the counter.

Two modern arcades, which are more like shopping complexes, are **Centrepoint** and **The Walk**. Their shops specialise in fashions for the young.

Along The Causeway, off the mall, is the **Spaghetti Bazaar**, where you can enjoy large helpings of spaghetti served with a small loaf of bread and a pot of butter.

McKillop Street is one of the lanes which have been made into a pedestrian-only thoroughfare. On the corner of this pretty street, with its trees and lanterns, and Bourke Street is **Kozminsky's**, a well-respected

SHOPPING

shop for antique jewellery; and in McKillop Street itself, **Discurio** have a wonderful range of classical records, cassettes and CDs, and a most knowledgeable staff. **The Compleat Angler** sells all the equipment a fisherman would need.

Almost opposite McKillop Street, off Bourke Street and between Elizabeth and Queen Streets, is **Hardware Street**, which has been given a facelift with brick paving. Here you will find the Italian café, **Campari**, which has long been a popular place for luncheons for the smart office set. Service is swift, and you can sit very happily at the bar if you are alone.

Also in Hardware Street are shops which sell skiing, bushwalking and adventure equipment, such as **Auski**, **Kathmandu**, **Alpine Ski Centre** and, around the corner in Little Bourke Street, the well-known **Paddy Pallin**, which sells adventure outdoor wear.

Collins Street has some of the city's most impressive shopping venues. The Hyatt on Collins includes a landscaped atrium called **Collins Chase**, roofed with a vaulted glass dome and offering two levels of exclusive shopping boutiques and food court. Walk through the glass doors from Collins Street and you enter a beautifully light and airy interior, glistening with marble. The luxury shops include internationally known designer names—Louis Vuitton luggage, Piaget watches—and local names, with mostly imported fashions: Raphael, Ipanema (unusual designs for women) and John J Moore

(menswear with such exclusive labels as Ermenegildo Zegna). Downstairs is the Food Court, with a wide choice including Japanese *sushi*, home-made pasta, tortes and salads. Upstairs is the spacious foyer of the Hyatt Hotel, with its gleaming Italian golden marble.

The elegant **Georges**, 162–168 Collins Street, is Melbourne's most exclusive department store. Once it was old-fashioned in décor, with appropriately old-fashioned staff and service. In recent years it has been modernised into a glittering marble and mirrored establishment, though the fine old façade remains. Its fashions include top European designers such as Valentino and Christian Dior. Walk through to its Hostess store in Little Collins Street, to see luxury items for the home. Look out for antique furniture and fine tapestries from Portugal. **The Block Arcade**, at 274 Collins Street, is the most beautiful of all Melbourne's arcades, with its high domed glass ceiling and mosaic floor. It was built in 1892, inspired by the Galleria Vittoria in Milan, and has recently been restored and painted in warm red terracotta, biscuit and apricot. Some of the shops are copper fronted; some have painted ceilings. The **Hopetoun Tea Rooms** have been there since the arcade opened. In a little laneway, Block Place, a mixture of shops includes an elegant little eatery called **Rita's Café**, where interesting meals are served from 07.30 hrs. Next door is a takeaway, belonging to Rita, which sells delicious and healthy muesli cakes.

'Colonial style' accommodation brings a flavour of Victoria past

ACCOMMODATION

There is a wide range of accommodation within the centre of Melbourne, from luxury hotels to backpackers' lodgings, and costs vary to suit all budgets, from the very expensive hotels to inexpensive dormitories. There is no official rating system. Some properties provide special rates for stays of one week or longer.

A little further out in nearby suburbs, are smaller hotels, motels and caravan parks, some of which have camping areas. You can pitch your tent just six miles (10km) from the heart of the city (see **Camping** for further details).

Serviced apartments are becoming more popular for those who prefer self-catering and if you are staying longer than a few days, it can be cheaper. Several luxury hotels now have apartment-style rooms, so you can either use hotel services or be independent.

Visitors can also stay in an Australian home in the city or the country, or spend time on a farm. Motels are the main type of accommodation when travelling around Victoria, and there are motel-style hotels in the city and suburbs. They offer first-class en-suite units with modern amenities, including refrigerator and television. Most are single storey so that you can drive your car right to the door. Usually the

ACCOMMODATION

only meal served is breakfast, brought to the room, although some have a bistro attached, or outside barbecue areas where you can cook your own meal. Hotels or pubs in the suburbs are more for drinking than sleeping. Many older establishments have been refurbished, but still retain the old world style, and some restaurants, out of town, offer overnight accommodation, which can take away the worry of driving home after an evening of wining and dining.

The **Victour** Office is at 230 Collins Street, City (tel: 619 9444), and has lists of accommodation in Melbourne.

The Royal Automobile Club of Victoria (RACV) publishes a very detailed guide, *The Australian National Tourguide*, which covers all types of accommodation throughout Australia—de luxe hotels,

Country pubs, Victoria style, are likely to be renovated hotels

motels, caravan parks, holiday flats, serviced apartments, guest houses, holiday lodges, houseboat holidays and cruiser hire, classified by the affiliated Automobile Asssociations in each state. The Guide is available to non-members as well as members, and there is a charge. Automobile clubs who have reciprocal rights with the RACV can use the free accommodation booking service: RACV, 422 Little Collins Street, City (tel: 607 2137).

There are several motel chains where you can book ahead free from any member motel when touring, and which may have offices in your home country where you can book in advance. Vouchers will be refunded on your return home if you do not use them all. One such company is Flag International Ltd, 132 Bank Street, South Melbourne (tel: 698 7777).

Hotels

Super de luxe

Super de luxe hotels are of international standard, offering guest rooms and suites with *en suite* bathrooms, bath robes, hair dryers, television, radio, mini bars and direct international dialling.

Two of the most luxurious hotels are situated at the Paris end of Collins Street. The grand Italian marble foyer sets the luxury theme for the **Hyatt on Collins** at 123 Collins Street (main hotel entrance from Russell Street; tel: 657 1234). Escalators from street level take you to the spacious foyer; and the hotel is noted for its leisure facilities, including such luxuries as a swimming pool, spa, sauna, gym and tennis courts.

The Regent, Collins Place, 25 Collins Street (tel: 653 0000), has the most stunning views from each of its 363 guest rooms, which are situated from the 36th to the 50th storey. You can see the whole layout of Melbourne as far as Port Phillip Bay and the Dandenongs. The hotel has a Health Department, free to all guests, with fully qualified instructors offering personal fitness programmes.

Rockman's Regency Hotel, on the corner of Exhibition and Lonsdale Streets (tel: 662 3900), is a small hotel with a great reputation. It has a warm personality, which has attracted guests such as Bob Hope and Shirley Bassey. The Regency Bar is open only to house guests and customers using the restaurant.

All rooms have a separate dressing room, and luxury accessories, even an umbrella. There is complimentary fruit and morning/evening newspapers, and facilities include a swimming pool and solarium. Situated in Spring Street is a

Luxury is the keyword at Melbourne's elegant Hyatt on Collins

ACCOMMODATION

completely different style of
hotel. **The Windsor**, 100 Spring
Street (tel: 653 0653), is one of the
grand old hotels of the world. It
has been magnificently restored
to its Victorian splendour, and all
190 rooms are decorated in old
world style. The Victorian suites
are furnished with antiques, and
the rooms have walk-in
wardrobes. Margaret Thatcher
and Rudolf Nureyev have been
among the guests and Dame
Edna Everage/Barrie
Humphries stay here on their
regular visits to Melbourne, and
the Grand Dining Room is the
most lavish in Melbourne. The
hotel belongs to the Oberoi
Hotel organisation.

Luxury
The new **Eden on the Yarra**, on
the corner of Flinders and
Spencer Streets (tel: 650 6111), is
right on the river. It is part of the

*A queen among grand hotels: the
Windsor, restored to glory*

World Congress Centre and
ideal for those attending
conventions there. Two
restaurants and three bars.
The **Hilton on the Park**, 192
Wellington Parade (on the
corner with Clarendon Street)
East Melbourne (tel: 419 3311), is
in a lovely position, opposite the
Fitzroy and Treasury Gardens,
and only a short tram ride from
the city centre. The Melbourne
Cricket Ground is across the
road, and some of the guest
rooms open onto the swimming
pool area.
The **Hotel Como**, 630 Chapel
Street, South Yarra (tel:
824 0400), is a superb small hotel,
set within the new Como
complex. All of the 107 guest
rooms are suites, mostly
spacious self-contained

apartments with kitchens, dining and sitting rooms. Some have separate offices, and there are original works of art especially commissioned from Australian painters, sculptors and ceramicists in each suite. Some have their own traditional Japanese gardens and extra deep baths, and there is a rooftop swimming pool, sauna and gym. In the club lounge complimentary continental breakfast and complimentary pre-dinner drinks are served and there is an all-day snack and beverage service, and although there is no dining room or restaurant, there is a special in-house dining service with Maxim's, one of Melbourne's top restaurants next door. Each suite has a direct telephone line for ordering a meal, or you can book a table in the restaurant itself. **Menzies at Rialto**, 495 Collins Street (tel: 620 9111), is part of the modern Rialto complex which has the tallest office building in Melbourne, but the hotel itself is behind the loveliest old Venetian Gothic façade dating back to 1892 with arched windows and ornate carving. The guest rooms have doors leading on to the striking 10-storey open atrium.

The Parkroyal is at 562 St Kilda Road (tel: 529 8888), close to the 18-hole Albert Park public golf course. It has an excellent dining room, bistro and rooftop spa and sauna.

The **Southern Cross**, 131 Exhibition Street (tel: 653 0221), is very conveniently situated in the centre of the city, and has recently been refurbished. **The Travelodge**, situated on the corner of St Kilda Road and Park Street, (tel: 699 4833), is near the city centre and conveniently placed for trams. It is near the Royal Botanic Gardens.

Moderate
Three hotels near each other in the city centre are the **Bryson**, 186 Exhibition Street (tel: 662 0511), **Noahs Hotel**, corner of Little Bourke Street and Exhibition Street (tel: 662 0511), and the **Château Melbourne**, 131 Lonsdale Street (tel: 663 3161). **The Sheraton** at 13 Spring Street (tel: 650 5000), overlooks the Treasury Gardens. In South Yarra, opposite Fawkner Park, is the **Albany Motor Inn**, Toorak Road and Millswyn Street (tel: 266 4485).

The **Old Melbourne**, 5 Flemington Road, North Melbourne (tel: 329 9344), has a flagstone central courtyard and decorative iron balconies. There are three restaurants, two bars, a gym, sauna and 24-hour room service. The attractive Georgian-style **Rathdowne International Motel**, 49 Rathdowne Street, Carlton (tel: 662 1388), is opposite the Carlton Gardens, (known as the Exhibition Gardens). Another motel is the **Downtowner**, which is right in the heart of Carlton at 66 Lygon Street (tel: 663 5555). The **Royal Parade Motor Inn** is in one of Melbourne's most beautiful streets, 441 Royal Parade, Parkville (tel: 380 9221), near the Hume Highway which leads to Sydney, and is within walking distance of the Royal Melbourne Zoo.

Although it no longer has accommodation, **Mac's Hotel**,

ACCOMMODATION

34 Franklin Street, is an interesting place to see. Now a drinking establishment, it is considered to be the oldest hotel in Melbourne. It was opened in 1855 and named after its first proprietor, James McMillan. It originally served as a terminus for coaches travelling to the goldfields, and offered a special lock-up for the gold and accommodation for members of the gold escort. The hotel was nearly destroyed on 11 November 1880, the day bushranger Ned Kelly was hanged. Emotions ran so high that one of the biggest fights seen in Melbourne broke out, which nearly wrecked the hotel.

Small is still stylish where Melbourne's hotels are concerned

Budget
The **City Square Motel**, with only 24 rooms, is tucked away amid the shops and banks at 67 Swanston Street (tel: 654 7011), opposite the City Square. Two other conveniently placed hotels are **City Limits Motel** at 20 Little Bourke Street (tel: 662 2544), and **Crossley Lodge** at 51 Little Bourke Street.

Georgian Court is in a pretty street in East Melbourne, at 21–25 George Street (tel: 419 6353). There are shared facilities, and breakfast is included in the tariff.

The **Victoria Hotel**, 215 Little Collins Street, City (tel: 653 0441), a turn-of-the-century hotel, is in an ideal location for a low-cost hotel. Some of its rooms do not have private facilities.

The Meeting Place is one of the latest ideas in combining accommodation and an eating establishment within a bistro and bar complex, at 319 Elizabeth Street, City (tel: 602 2888).
YWCA Family Motel, 489 Elizabeth Street, City (tel: 329 5188), has rooms with *en suite* shower and toilet, as well as a television lounge, sauna, laundry and heated pool. It is very popular, so booking in advance is advisable. Also in Elizabeth Street at 441 is **Rendezvous City Guesthouse** (tel: 429 7635), with hot and cold water and tea- and coffee-making facilities in each room.

Boutique Hotels
Magnolia Court, 101 Powlett Street, East Melbourne (tel: 419 4222), is in one of the prettiest streets in the area. Rooms have private facilities, direct-dial telephones, hair dryers and heated spa pool.
The Tilba, 30 Toorak Road and Domain Street (tel: 267 8844), is a beautifully restored Victorian mansion with rooms appropriately furnished to match that era, and communal reading and sitting rooms. It stands opposite the lovely Fawkner Park. Breakfast is included in the tariff. Moderate.

Serviced Apartments
Gordon Place, 24 Little Bourke Street, City (tel: 663 5355), is a historic building classified by the National Trust; beautifully furnished studio, one- and two-bedroomed apartments. You are welcomed with complimentary delicacies like pâté, cheese and biscuits, and facilities include a salt-water swimming pool, spa,

sauna and gym, a bistro and garden courtyard restaurant.
Oakford Fairways at 32 Queens Road (tel: 267 6511) has one or two bedrooms and penthouses. There is a tennis court, landscaped pool and across the road is Albert Park Lake 18-hole golf course. **Oakford Apartments**, 631 Punt Road, South Yarra, have similar facilities.
There are nine different Oakford properties in the heart of Melbourne as well as properties in South Melbourne and South Yarra.
South Yarra Hill Suites, 14 Murphy Street, South Yarra (tel: 268 8222), are situated in a most attractive street, close to Toorak Road at the centre of the South Yarra shopping centre. One- and two-bedroomed apartments, and three-bedroom de luxe in a garden setting. Some basic essentials such as cereal, milk and spreads are provided free of charge.

Backpackers
Dormitories, twins and double accommodation are available at the **Backpackers' Inns**. There are two in the city at 197 Bourke Street (tel: 650 4379) and 230 Russell Street (tel: 663 7862), and another at St Kilda at 24 Mitford Street (tel: 525 4355) near bayside beaches. St Kilda has plenty of cheap eating establishments. More backpackers' accommodation can be found at the **Royal Artillery Hotel**, 616 Elizabeth Street (tel: 347 3917). Remember that backpacker accommodation can sometimes be a crowded and noisy affair.

ACCOMMODATION

Pubs, Homes and Farms

If you want more of an opportunity to meet the local people, try staying at a family home in the suburbs; or at a farm, where you can choose from a wide range of activities, such as harvesting and haymaking, shearing or horse-riding; or at one of the pubs, most of which are recently renovated old hotels.

Book through your travel agent or through one of the specialist organisations:

Australian Home Accommodation and **Australian Pubstays**, first floor, Albert Park Hotel, 83 Dundas Place, Albert Park (tel: 696 0422). Farms are subject to a rating system, denoted by a kangaroo symbol; and pubs are categorised into four standards, denoted by the Rufus Fantail, an Australian bird noted for its friendliness.

The Host Farms Association of Victoria also has a wide choice of properties on its books, which can be reserved through **Victour**, 230 Collins Street, City (tel: 619 9444).

Out of town

Melburnians like to go away from the city for the weekend and there is a wide choice of places to stay. The most luxurious places are the most popular, where the ambience and the food come before the actual accommodation. Overnight accommodation in a delightful cottage is available at **Cotswold House**, Blackhill Road, Menzies Creek (tel: 754 7884), which has the highest reputation for its creative and original cuisine. The simple rustic setting overlooks the garden with geese and ducks wandering across the lawn. Expensive.

Degany Country House Hotel, Nepean Highway, Portsea (tel: (059) 844 000), and its restaurant, Two Faces, is a unique combination. They have the only double accreditation of Relais et Châteaux status and Relais Gourmand listing, in the southern hemisphere. The house was built as a private home in the 1920s in the style of a castle, and has previously been a hospital and a convent. There is a pool, tennis courts and golf course, and it is near bayside and ocean beaches.

The **Queenscliff Hotel**, 16 Gellibrand Street, Queenscliff (tel: (052) 52 1982). Opened in 1888, this beautiful old hotel with its graceful and elegant arches and columns has been restored to its original glory. There is an exquisite entrance hall, sitting room, 25 bedrooms and a conservatory and garden courtyard, (see **Excursions**, page 47).

Youth Hostels

Youth hostels welcome members of the International Youth Hostel movement. There is accommodation for 300. No alcohol is allowed, and there is a 23.00 hrs curfew. For reservations, contact 205 King Street, City (tel: 670 7991).

Two hostels in the inner suburb of North Melbourne are at 500 Abbotsford Street (tel: 328 2880) and 76 Chapman Street (tel: 328 3595). Overflow members can stay at the University of Melbourne colleges during vacation periods.

NIGHTLIFE AND ENTERTAINMENT

There is no shortage of entertainment in Melbourne, and the nightlife is lively and varied. See the **Directory** for details of **Entertainment Information**.

Cinemas

There are many multi-cinema complexes in Bourke and Russell Streets, in the city, showing the latest commercial releases. Film showings are listed in the daily newspapers under the headings of the cinema companies: Hoyts, Greater Union and Village centres. Cinemas which concentrate on European films

Reflections of a city by night: Melbourne lights up after dark

include the **Kino Cinema**, Collins Place, 45 Collins Street (tel: 650 2100); and **State Film Centre**, 1 Macarthur Street, East Melbourne (tel: 651 1490) which specialises in documentaries and art films. **Chinatown Cinema**, 108 Lonsdale Street (tel: 662 3465) has films from Hong Kong and Taiwan in Cantonese, with English subtitles.
In the suburbs: **Brighton Bay Twin Cinemas**, 294 Bay Street, Brighton (tel: 596 3590); **Rivoli Twin Cinemas**, 200 Camberwell Road, Hawthorn (tel: 882 1221)

NIGHTLIFE AND ENTERTAINMENT

and **Longford Cinema**, 55 Toorak Road, South Yarra (tel: 267 2700).

Concerts

The **Victorian Arts Centre**, St Kilda Road (tel: 1-1366) is the focus of Melbourne's cultural life. Here you can find concerts, opera, ballet and theatre, all housed in one complex near the river. The **Melbourne Concert Hall**, with its stunning red plush interior, is 'tuned' so that its acoustics can be varied to suit all types of music. The acoustic banners and perspex shells, which can be moved to alter the sound, are part of the spectacular décor, which reflects the colour and environment of the Australian continent. The concrete walls are like slices of earth, painted in colours and patterns found in Australia's mineral and gemstone deposits. The hall's organ, built by Casavant Frères of Quebec, is free-standing and encased in oak; communication between the organist and the stage is by closed circuit television. The Arts Centre is home of the **Melbourne Symphony Orchestra**, which gives regular concerts, and is the top venue too for visiting overseas musicians.

Chamber music concerts are occasionally arranged at the Hall by **Musica Viva**, who also give performances at the University of Melbourne's Faculty of Music (tel: 240 9731).

Contemporary Music

It has been said that there are more night-clubs in Melbourne than in New York—with all the latest modern music, disco and live bands. **Metro**, 20–30 Bourke Street, City (tel: 663 4288) is the largest. **Chasers**, 386 Chapel Street, South Yarra (tel: 241 6615) plays disco music and **ID'S**, 132 Greville Street, Prahran (tel: 529 6900), has anything from jazz to country music, soul to rock.

Melbourne Concert Hall's organ is a treat for the eyes and for the ears

NIGHTLIFE AND ENTERTAINMENT

Bookings advisable.
The Ivy, 147 Flinders Lane, City (tel: 650 5377), attracts a broad group of people. Four floors, cocktail bar, restaurant. Live entertainment after midnight. There is live music in many hotels on most nights of the week. The **Royal Derby Hotel**, 446 Brunswick Street, North Fitzroy (tel: 417 2321), is popular. Jazz—is everywhere! The most sophisticated venue is the foyer of the **Studio Theatre** in the **Victorian Arts Centre**, Friday and Saturday 23.00–02.00 hrs (cover charge).
Hotels include **The Limerick Arms**, 364 Clarendon Street, South Melbourne (tel: 690 2626) and the **Museum Hotel**, 293 La Trobe Street, City (tel: 670 0128), where the Victorian Jazz Club organises sessions.
Free outdoor concerts, from symphony to rock, are held in the **Sidney Myer Music Bowl** in the King's Domain.
The **National Gallery Great Hall**, on St Kilda Road, and the **Town Hall**, in Swanston Street, often have free Sunday concerts. In the summer there is free lunchtime entertainment in the city squares and gardens.

Theatres
Theatre productions cover the whole spectrum, from big shows to intimate, from comedy to experimental and theatre restaurants.
There are three auditoriums in the **Victorian Arts Centre**. The largest is the **State Theatre**, which seats 2,000. It is used mainly by the Australian Opera, the Victorian State Opera and the Australian Ballet, which has

The renovated Princess Theatre

its headquarters in Melbourne. The Melbourne Theatre Company plays in the **Playhouse**, and the smaller theatre is the **Studio**, which is used for experimental theatre productions.
Apart from the theatres at the Victorian Arts Centre, the best known are the **Athenaeum Theatre**, 188 Collins Street, City (tel: 650 1977); **Comedy Theatre**, 240 Exhibition Street, City (tel: 662 2222), which stages popular plays; and **Russell Street Theatre**, 19 Russell Street, City (tel: 654 4000). The top company, the Melbourne Theatre Company, performs here as well as in the Victorian Arts Centre. The newly renovated **Princess**

Theatre, 163 Spring Street, City (tel: 663 4159) features the 'big' shows, such as *Les Misérables*; you can take daily tours of this historic theatre (tel: 662 2911). The top theatre specialising in comedy is **The Last Laugh** 64 Smith Street, Collingwood (tel: 419 8600).

Tikki and John's, 169 Exhibition Street, City (tel: 663 1754), is a long-established theatre restaurant.

You can buy theatre tickets at half price on the day of the performance from **Half-Tix** a stall in the Bourke Street Mall, between Swanston Street and Elizabeth Street. This includes drama, comedy, musicals, dance and opera (tel: 650 9420, recorded information; or 649 8888).

WEATHER AND WHEN TO GO

Melbourne has four distinct seasons: spring (September to November); summer (December to February); autumn (March to May) and winter (June to August).

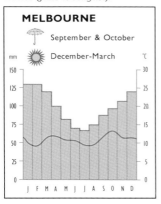

MELBOURNE

September & October

December-March

Autumn, in March and April, is a beautiful time of the year. Days are usually sunny and windless and the city is ablaze with autumn leaves from the many deciduous trees. Spring is also attractive, with blossom, rhododendrons and azaleas. Melbourne has a mild, temperate climate, though there can be snow in the Dandenongs. Average temperatures for the seasons are:

Spring 15°C (59°F)
Summer 25°C (77°F)
Autumn 17°C (63°F)
Winter 13°C (55°F)

Be prepared for the sudden changes of weather which are one of Melbourne's famous characteristics!

The coldest month is July, when temperatures can drop close to freezing.

Rainfall, which has an annual average of 25 inches (658mm), is evenly distributed throughout the year.

HOW TO BE A LOCAL

With so many Australian television soap operas being shown around the world, there are not many surprises about Australians! Their informality, speech and greetings have become well known—Paul Hogan's 'G'day' is familiar across the globe—and you do not even have to wait to come to Australia to have a cold can, or tube, or tinny of Foster's, because the Melbourne-born lager is now being exported! But like all nationalities, Australians are not always as they are portrayed. You will hear some Melburnians say 'G'day', but there would be

A calm kangaroo lends an ear to one of Melbourne's young visitors

more saying 'Hello' or 'Good morning'!

Melburnians are reputed to be the most formal of Australians—in speech, dress and entertainment, which often takes the form of dinner parties in their homes or their clubs. Melburnians are considered to be sincere with invitations. They will not generally say 'You must come to dinner', without intending to follow the offer with a definite date. When invited to dinner in a home, you usually take a small gift, such as a bottle of wine and/or a bunch of flowers or chocolates for the hostess.

But things are becoming more informal and casual. Once top restaurants would not allow men to dine without wearing a tie and jacket, but today fashions decree otherwise.

The pronunciation of Melbourne itself marks out the real locals. They tend to emphasise the first syllable: '*Mel*bun'; whereas visitors put more emphasis on the last: 'Mel*bourne*'.

Australia still has not shaken off the label of male chauvinism, and women will often find that different social rules apply to each sex.

It is customary when a group of males are drinking at a bar for each one to 'shout' (buy) a round of drinks. If you are a man you would not want to leave without doing so! In a bar or at a private party, Australian males have the reputation of standing together rather than mixing with women. It is a 'tradition' which is changing—a little.

A lone male passenger in a taxi usually sits in front next to the driver; a lone woman passenger will sit in the back. It has long been the lot of a woman traveller to have to eat or drink by herself. Once, in the 'old days' in Australia, women could not go into a bar in a hotel, even with a man. But recent licensing laws in Melbourne are making it more and more comfortable for women to eat and drink where they like, and women travelling alone have virtually no restrictions on where they can go in Melbourne.

PERSONAL PRIORITIES

Melbourne is a modern city with ample shopping facilities, and you should have no problem finding items such as babies' nappies, tampons or contraceptives.

Shops stock familiar, international brand names and pharmacies sell tampons and other 'feminine hygiene' products over the counter. Contraceptives are available and condoms are on display. For pharmacies which open long hours, see the **Directory**, under **Pharmacies**, page 120.

CHILDREN

Being a city of parks and gardens, Melbourne is a great

Drinking can be a smart affair, particularly in hotel bars

Children can sail the seas without raising anchor on the Polly Woodside

place to take children. Among the attractions which may particularly appeal to them is the **Children's Museum**, within the Museum of Victoria, 328 Swanston Street with activities and hands-on exhibits. In the Museum of Victoria there are some displays that could interest children, including a number of interesting live exhibits, such as snakes, in the Victorian country life exhibit! (admission free; open Monday to Sunday 10.00–17.00 hrs).

During school holidays the **Performing Arts Museum**, at the Victorian Arts Centre, has exhibitions to appeal to children (see page 34).

Other museums which could be of interest: **The Melbourne Fire Brigade Museum**, with all its old fire-fighting equipment. It is next to the modern fire station, with gleaming red fire engines in full view.

The **Maritime Museum**'s centrepiece, the barque *Polly Woodside*, is moored in the water, and children can clamber

CHILDREN

over this restored sailing ship and ride on a flying fox, which is set up in the Museum's grounds. In the summer there are many entertainments in the parks and gardens. Such well known stories as *Wind in the Willows* are acted out in the **Royal Botanic Gardens**, or other park venues.

Children's bicycles can be hired for rides on the cycling track along the Yarra River.

The numerous parks provide plenty of running space for children. There are swans and ducks to feed in the Royal Botanic Gardens, and areas for picnic snacks.

At the **Royal Melbourne Zoo** (see page 38) there is the opportunity to see animals and birds from all around the world, as well as some Australian varieties; and at the **Healesville Sanctuary** (see page 45) children can see all the unique Australian species at close quarters.

In the Dandenongs a special attraction for children is **Puffing Billy**, a small steam train which runs on a narrow gauge line through forests, fern gullies and across a trestle bridge on its round trip starting from Belgrave (tel: 754 6800 timetable or 870 8411, recorded information).

Sovereign Hill at Ballarat, is ideal for an out of town excursion. There is plenty of fascination in the old shops and the people dressed in period costume, and

Puffing Billy *steams ahead*

children can pan for gold or
have a ride on a horse-drawn
coach (see page 41).

The **Billa Billa Homestead**,
Howell Road, Gilderoy, 50 miles
(80km) east of Melbourne, offers
a day out in the High Country
seeing wombats and kangaroos
and taking part in the activities of
a typical Australian farm: horse
riding, fishing or four-wheel
driving (tel: (059) 66 7244).

And **Victoria's Farm Shed**,
Princes Highway, Tynonig 3813,
43 miles (70km) east of
Melbourne, has farm animal
parades and shearing, milking
and sheepdog demonstrations.
(Open daily; shows
10.30–14.30 hrs April to October,
10.30–13.30 hrs November to
March. Free admission).

TIGHT BUDGET

You can see and do a lot around
Melbourne for little, or even no
cost.

Information on the City is free
from **Victour**, 230 Collins Street.
You can choose from shelves full
of brochures covering all
attractions in Melbourne and
Victoria; a tourist map and a
current weekly *What's On in
Melbourne*—are all free.

You can buy one ticket, an all-
day travelcard, for use on either
tram, train and bus. It allows you
to pop off and on whenever you
like. Trams may be slower, but
they are easy to use and go to, or
near, most sights.

You see a great deal by walking
around the streets of Melbourne:
the different styles of
architecture, monuments,
memorials, decorative drinking
fountains, statues and squares of

Go to the beach to escape the crowds

attractive houses (especially in
Carlton); and of course there are
the beautifully landscaped parks
and gardens. Swimming and
sun-bathing on the bayside
beaches are also free.
Cathedrals and churches are
free to visit, and the **Museum of
Victoria** is free. Classical music
can be heard free at concerts
given by music students and
professionals at the **University of
Melbourne** during term. You can
sit on the lawns near the **Myer
Music Bowl** during the summer
to hear all types of concerts held
there, at no charge. Many pubs
have live, loud bands playing
which you can enjoy for the
price of a beer—or two. Some of
these venues have backpacker
accommodation.

St Kilda has cheap
accommodation and eating
establishments. Some of the
cafés there have emphasis on
wholefood, organic, vegetarian

SPECIAL EVENTS

or macrobiotic, which is cheap and imaginative: try **Rasa's Vegie Bar**, 25 Blessington Street, St Kilda, or **Wild Rice**, 211 Barkly Street, St Kilda. In the nearby suburb of Elwood the **Café Tarrango** at 15 Ormond Road gives value for money.

If you are buying food you cannot beat the **Queen Victoria Market** for cheapness. Around closing time, at noon or a bit later, boxes and bags of fruit and vegetables are almost given away for only a couple of dollars. Clothes are cheap there, too, especially on Sundays.

Coles, in Bourke Street, have good, cheap basic goods such as clothes, crockery and stationery, as well as a family restaurant.

The **Travellers' Aid Society of Victoria**, 169 Swanston Street, offers low cost meals, showers, lockers, ironing room (open Monday to Friday 08.00–17.30 hrs; Saturday 10.00–16.00 hrs). There is also a branch at Spencer Street Railway Station (open Monday to Friday 08.30–20.30 hrs).

If you want to travel to other states in Australia, express coaches are the cheapest way to go (see **Directory**, under **Public Transport**, page 121).

SPECIAL EVENTS

There is an increasing number of festivals in and around Melbourne. Most relate to music, food or gardens. Some are successful enough to become annual events; others are limited to a certain area. They are all well advertised in the media. Melbourne's main events and festivals include:

Bright colours and a carnival spirit at the Moomba Festival

January

Melbourne Summer Music Festival
Australian Open Tennis Championships, a Grand Slam event

March

Moomba: a long-established, carnival-style festival, which includes water sports and entertainment on the river and a parade of colourful floats through the city streets. *Moomba* is an

Aboriginal word meaning 'let's get together and have fun'.

April

Anzac Day (25th): Commemorates the war dead. There is a march of ex-servicemen and women through the streets, ending at the Shrine of Remembrance (see page 37), where a solemn ceremony is held. The date commemorates the landing of Australian and New Zealand forces at Gallipoli, Turkey during World War I. It is a national public holiday, and the dead of all wars are remembered at similar services in cities and towns throughout Australia.

June

International Film Festival
Official opening of snow skiing season in Victoria

September

Melbourne International Festival of the Arts: a broad spectrum of music, dance, theatre and art, with Australian and international companies and celebrities taking part
Royal Melbourne Show: a display of the best agriculture

and livestock that country Victoria has to offer Australian Rules Football Grand Final: the whole city gets caught up in footy fever!

November

Spring Racing Carnival, which includes the Melbourne Cup, the horse race which brings the country to a standstill. Just about everyone stops work, or pleasure, to watch the race on television, if they are not at the course!

Lygon Street Festival: this street with the Italian air, in Carlton, is closed off for the weekend for musical and other entertainments

Spanish Festival, Johnson Street, Fitzroy

December

Carols by Candelight at the Myer Music Bowl, and other parks, to celebrate Christmas.

SPORT

Melburnians, like most Australians, are great lovers of sport, both as spectators and participators. In winter, football fever takes over the city—Australian Rules Football, that is. In summer, Test cricket draws the crowds, especially if it is an England-Australia season, as do the Australian Open Tennis Championships, and horse racing, where Melburnians can have the two-way advantage of being spectators and participators in another love of their life: gambling. Most people like, at least once in their lives, to attend the greatest of all horse races, the Melbourne Cup. The people of Melbourne have

virtually the whole spectrum of sports in which to participate; even if they are based not right in the city, the smallness of the state ensures that they will not be far away. Snow skiing for the weekend is easily accessible and popular; surfing beaches are a couple of hours' drive away. If you want something more adventurous, there is rock-climbing, gliding, bush-walking or sailboard riding—or whatever your interest may be.

Cricket

The cricket season is from November to March, and the main venue for matches is the **Melbourne Cricket Ground (MCG)**. This is the Melbourne ground for the Test matches played between Australia and visiting overseas teams from England, the West Indies, New Zealand, India, Pakistan and Sri Lanka.

One day matches are also held here during the day and under lights at night. You will see local cricket matches being played in many parks, which is about as near an English village green as you will see in Australia. The main local competition is the Sheffield Shield, played between teams from the different Australian states at the MCG. Test match tickets are available at the gates on the day of the match, or can be pre-booked through BASS Booking Agents. Further information from the **Australian Cricket Board** (tel: 654 3977).

MCG: tram 28, 29, 40, 42, 75 or 76 from Flinders Street to stop 16; or train from Flinders Street Station to Richmond or Jolimont Station.

Victorian football is a home-grown game with a widening appeal

Football

Australian Rules Football (Aussie Rules) originated in Victoria in the 1850s, and has been described as a cross between rugby, soccer and Gaelic football. It has also been referred to by non-Victorians as 'aerial ping-pong'. But in recent years its popularity has spread outside Victoria, and teams from other Australian states now take part in the major competition organised by the Victorian Football League (VFL). The season is from March to mid-September. It has also gained a wide television audience throughout Australia. Team names are of the different suburbs, including Carlton, Hawthorn, Collingwood, Essendon, Fitzroy and St Kilda. They are known by symbols such as hawks, magpies, tigers and bulldogs. The two highest scoring teams play in the Grand Final, a great spectacle, with around 100,000 spectators. Main matches are played throughout the season at the **Victorian Football League Park (VFL)**, on Friday nights commencing 19.35 hrs, Saturday from 14.00 hrs and Sunday from 14.05 hrs. Tickets can be obtained at the gates before the

SPORT

matches. Grand Final tickets are sold out before the day and are very difficult to buy. They are mostly allocated to clubs for distribution. The Grand Final is televised live and is a great spectacle, even if you are not a follower of the game.

Newspapers are full of it: so much is written and said and shown about this game that an anti-football league has been formed!

Further information on Aussie Rules from the **Victorian Football League** VFL Park, Mulgrave (tel: 654 1244).

Golf

Major golf tournaments have become more and more popular as a spectator sport in recent years. Australian and world championships are held in Melbourne during January and February at top courses, including **Royal Melbourne Golf Club**, Cheltenham Road, Black Rock (tel: 598 6755) and **Huntingdale Golf Club**, Windsor Avenue, Oakleigh (tel: 579 3674). Royal Melbourne is regarded as one of the top golf courses in the world. Information about obtaining tickets for the major events is available from **The Victorian Golf Association** (tel: 553 3211).

Horse Racing

Melburnians, young and old, are great racegoers. The first horse racing club was established in 1838, only three years after the city was founded. There are meetings in Melbourne and metropolitan and country courses on nearly every day of the week but Sundays, when meetings are not usually held.

The four main race courses in Melbourne are **Flemington**, run by the Victorian Racing Club (VRC) and **Caulfield**, **Sandown Park** and **Moonee Valley**, run by the Victoria Amateur Turf Club (VATC). All have excellent spectator facilities, and you will not hear better or faster race calling! The often maligned slow Australian drawl is never evident in the speech of race callers.

Major meetings in Melbourne are held on Saturdays, but there are some on weekdays, and occasionally evening meetings are also held in summer. Horse racing receives great coverage in the media and you will always be able to find out where the meetings are being held.

Horse racing is also the most popular gambling sport. You can bet on and off the course. On the course there are licensed bookmakers, and the government-controlled **Totalisator Agency Board** (TAB), which are also situated in the city and suburbs. There is hardly an Australian town without its TAB. The betting system on the TAB includes win and place and multiple forms covering the first three placed horses.

Further information on race meetings and betting is available from the **TAB**, 1 Queens Road, Melbourne (tel: 268 2100), open Monday to Saturday 08.45–18.30 hrs (after hours racing enquiries, tel: 268 2179; telephone betting enquiries: 268 2323).

Public transport to the race courses:

Caulfield Race Course, Station Street, Caulfield: tram 3 from

Swanston Street. Dandenong, or Frankston line train from Flinders Street Station to Caulfield Station.

Flemington Race Course, Epsom Road, Flemington: special race trains leave from Flinders Street Station and go right into the course on the days meetings are held.

Moonee Valley Race Course, McPherson Street, Moonee Ponds: tram 59 from Elizabeth Street to Moonee Ponds Junction.

Melbourne Cup

At 14.40 hrs on the first Tuesday of November each year, Australia comes to a standstill. It is the official starting time for the Melbourne Cup, one of the world's great horse races. The day is declared an official public holiday in Melbourne, and throughout Australia people stop work to listen to or watch the Cup on radio or television. The first Melbourne Cup was held in 1861, and it is now Australia's richest horse race, with prize money of over two million dollars. Held at Flemington Race Course, this is the highlight of the Spring Racing Carnival. Derby Day is on the Saturday prior to the Cup, and the final race is on the following Saturday.

Everything stops for the Melbourne Cup, a great sporting event

SPORT

Among past legends of the Cup, the horse that captured the imagination of the people more than any other was Phar Lap, who won in 1930. Phar Lap was a New Zealand horse, bought for only 160 guineas, and not very impressive at first. But he began to win races against all odds, and was taken to the US, where he won one race before dying suddenly and, some say, mysteriously. His heart is kept in the Science Museum in Canberra, and his body can be seen in the Museum of Victoria in Melbourne.

Tennis
Tennis is played all year round. In December and January, the Australian Open Tennis Championships, one of the four Grand Slam events, takes place at the **Flinders Park National Tennis Centre**, Batman Avenue (tel: 665 1244). During the second half of January the world's top men and women players, plus other sporting and show biz personalities attracted to the event, converge on Melbourne for this two-week clash on cement.

The Australian Open Championships are preceded in December by the smaller Victorian Tennis Open Championships, also at Flinders Park.

Participator Sports

Cycling
There has been a great increase in the number of cyclists in Melbourne, and more and more bicycle paths and lanes are being laid out. The most beautiful and easiest ride in the metropolitan area is on the

Melbourne is a cyclists' city, with plenty of lanes set aside

cycling track along the Yarra River, from the city to Toorak. At weekends it can be crowded as whole families come out and make a real occasion of it, with children on their own small bicycles or riding pillion behind their parents.

Bicycles for adults with baby carriers and tandems can be hired near **Princes Bridge** (tel: 801 2156, open: Monday to Friday 11.30–17.30 hrs; Saturday and Sunday 10.30–18.30 hrs). You can also hire them near **Como Park** (available from noon until dusk).

Further information on cycling in Melbourne can be obtained from **Bicycle Victoria**, 29–31 Somerset Place, City (tel: 670 9911).

Golf

There are 360 registered golf clubs in Victoria, and about 60 in the metropolitan area. There are about 25 public golf courses around Melbourne. These are especially busy at weekends, and some clubs have introduced advance bookings systems. It is advisable to check with the club. Public courses closest to the city are: **Albert Park Golf Course**, Queens Road (tel: 51 5588), **Royal Park Public Golf Course**, Poplar Road, Parkville (tel: 387 3585) and **Yarra Bend Kew and Fairfield Golf Course**, Park Road, Fairfield (tel: 481 0866). Further away, but very popular because it is opposite Melbourne's top private club, Royal Melbourne, is **Sandringham Golf Links**, Cheltenham Road, Cheltenham (tel: 598 3590). Further information from the

Victorian Golf Association (tel: 553 3211).

Horse Riding

You need to go to the country to experience great horse riding Australian style. And nothing could be more exciting than to ride on a **Lovick's Mountain Trail Safari** (tel: (057) 77 5510). The Lovicks have been horsemen for generations, and were among the top horsemen in the film *The Man from Snowy River*. The safaris will take you to Victoria's beautiful high country, beyond Mt Buller, a favoured ski resort in winter. There are weekend and up to eight-day safaris, beginning in October and continuing through the summer months.

Ice-skating

The **Sidney Myer Music Bowl**, King's Domain (tel: 617 8360) is iced over in winter from late April to late September (open: Monday and Tuesday 10.00–18.00 hrs; Wednesday to Saturday 10.00–22.00 hrs; Sunday 10.00–20.00 hrs). The **Olympic Ice Skating Centre**, 1080 Centre Road, Oakleigh (tel: 579 3755) has varying opening hours.

Skiing

The snowfields of Victoria are a three-hour or more drive from Melbourne. The official skiing season starts on the second Monday in June, and extends until September.

The three major skiing resorts are **Mt Buller**, 147 miles (237km) from Melbourne (tel: (057) 77 6977); **Falls Creek**, 234 miles (377km) from Melbourne (tel: (057) 58 3224) and **Mt Hotham via Bright**, 228 miles (367km) from

SPORT

You don't have to be an expert to enjoy Mount Buller's ski slopes

Melbourne (tel: (057) 59 3550). Mt Buller is noted for the variety of its downhill runs for beginners, intermediate and more experienced skiers. Four miles (6km) away is its 'twin', Mt Stirling, which offers the most extensive range of cross country trails in the southern hemisphere.

Falls Creek is a classic alpine village, where you can ski from the front door of your lodge. Mt Hotham's downhill slopes are for the more experienced skier. Five miles (8km) away is Dinner Plain Resort, whose unique architecture has made it one of Australia's award-winning alpine villages.

You can obtain further information from the **Victorian Ski Association**, 31 Coventry Street, South Melbourne (tel: 699 3292).

Surfing

Surfing beaches are a couple of hours' drive from Melbourne, but many are recommended for experienced swimmers and surfers only; rips and changing winds can make the waters dangerous, and conditions can change from smooth to rough in a matter of minutes. If waves are high and if there is a strong wind, inexperienced swimmers should stay near the shore.

There are some 30 beaches in Victoria patrolled by surf lifesavers on weekends and public holidays. The most popular beaches are also supervised over Christmas and during January.

Inexperienced swimmers and surfers should restrict themselves to *patrolled beaches* only. Swim between the flags. If you do get caught in the rip try not to panic; a rip is generally short. If you are in difficulties, raise your arm and a lifesaver will come to your aid.

On the east coast, **Gunnamatta** and **Portsea** are beaches for experienced swimmers and surfers.

On Phillip Island, **Woolamai** is for the experienced, and **Cowes** is a safe beach with one part restricted to swimmers.

On the west coast, **Jan Juc**, **Point Lonsdale**, **Barwon Heads**, **Bells Beach**, **Fairhaven** and the popular **Torquay** are for experienced surfers and swimmers. **Anglesea**, **Apollo Bay** and **Lorne** are generally considered to be safer.

For further information contact the **Australian Surf Riders Association** (tel: (052) 61 2907 or (052) 61 4460).

Ride the crest of a wave at St Kilda

Swimming

As well as the bayside beaches close to Melbourne, between Port Melbourne and St Kilda and from St Kilda to Portsea, there are many public swimming pools in Melbourne and the suburbs. Two of the more central pools are:

City Baths, 420 Swanston Street (tel: 663 5888) are open Monday to Friday 06.15–22.00 hrs, and Saturday and Sunday 08.00–18.00 hrs. You can catch any tram in Swanston Street and alight at the terminus (some trams go further along Swanston Street).

State Swimming Centre, Batman Avenue (tel: 654 2977) is used as a training pool, and the hours when it is open to the public are

SPORT

restricted and can change. It is advisable to check. Generally the pool is open to the public Monday to Friday 06.00–09.00 hrs, and Saturday and Sunday 11.00–15.00 hrs.

Tennis

Once everyone seemed to play tennis; then it went out of favour for some years. Tennis courts in private homes were turned into swimming pools, but are now being turned into tennis courts again! Many tennis courts can be hired.

Collingwood Indoor Tennis Centre, 100 Wellington Street, Collingwood (tel: 419 8911). Bright and airy indoor centre with five synthetic grass courts for hire. It is advisable to book in advance. *Open*: Monday to Friday 06.00 –around 22.00 hrs; Saturday and Sunday from 08.00 hrs.

Leggett's Tennis and Squash Centre, 132 Greville Street, Prahran (tel: 529 3322), has 10 outdoor tennis courts. *Open*: Monday to Friday 07.00–23.00 hrs; Saturday and Sunday 07.00–around 18.00 hrs.

National Tennis Centre, Flinders Park, Batman Avenue (tel: 665 1244). This is where the Australian Open is played. You cannot, unfortunately, play on the famed centre court, but you can play on courts on which many of the world's top tennis stars practice. Courts are closed during the two weeks of the Australian Open, in the second half of January. Otherwise, there are 13 outdoor and five indoor courts available for hire. *Open*: Monday to Friday 07.00–23.00 hrs; Saturday and Sunday 08.00–18.00 hrs. Tram 70 from Batman Avenue.

There are plenty of facilities for tennis, which has recently regained favour

DIRECTORY

Arriving	Entertainment	Police
Camping	Information	Post Office
Crime	Health Regulations	Public Transport
Customs Regulations	Holidays	Student and Youth
Disabled Facilities	Media	Travel
Driving	Money Matters	Telephones
Electricity	Opening Times	Time
Embassies and	Personal Safety	Tipping
Consulates	Pharmacies	Toilets
Emergency	Places of Worship	Tour Companies
Telephone Numbers		Tourist Offices

Arriving

All overseas travellers require a valid passport for entry into Australia. It must be valid for at least three months from your departure date. Everyone, except New Zealanders, requires a visa. Application forms for visas are obtainable from Australian consular offices (a visa is free, but may take several days to process). You need to present your passport; visa; an incoming passenger/immigration card; and a Customs, Quarantine and Wildlife Statement, which you will be given to complete on the aircraft. You also need a return or onward passenger ticket and may be asked for evidence of funds for the period of your stay. Basic visas are generally valid for six months.

By Air

When the aircraft touches down at Melbourne airport, the interior will be sprayed. You will be warned so that you can cover your face if you think it is necessary, but the spray is non-irritant and you should have no effect. Australia, being an isolated island, has long been kept free from many plant, animal and human disease which occur in other countries—such as yellow fever, rabies and foot and mouth disease, and it hopes to keep it that way. Spraying is a deterrent against importing such diseases, and is done at the first airport of entry only.

Australia is a long way from almost anywhere, even when you fly. The flight time from Britain is 21 hours or more; from Los Angeles 18 hours and from Tokyo nine hours.

It is a long and tiring flight, so choose loose, comfortable clothes, and drink plenty, to prevent dehydration (not necessarily alcohol, which could give you an even higher effect!). All international flights arrive at Melbourne Airport, which is 14 miles (22 kilometres) northwest of Melbourne. Once through official formalities, trolleys are available to carry baggage, for a charge. There are machines, which will change some foreign money, but it is always wise to bring a small amount of Australian currency with you. Your baggage may be searched, even if you go through the 'Nothing to Declare' gate. Once

DIRECTORY

The Port of Melbourne is the major cargo port of Australia

through customs you pass through to the arrival hall. If you are making your own way, there are telephones, car rental offices and signs for taxis. There is an express bus, Sky Bus (tel: 663 1400), which takes you to the city, and costs about one-third of a taxi fare. It is a pleasant drive along the Tullamarine freeway to the city, which takes around 35 minutes, depending on the flow of the traffic.

An airport tax is payable on departure.

Interstate flights: domestic flights between states throughout Australia also come into Tullamarine Airport.

The main two airlines are Australian Airlines and Ansett. It is expensive to fly within Australia; when you are booking your flight to Australia, enquire at your travel agency about interstate flights for overseas visitors—you will fly more cheaply than the locals.

In addition, regional airlines

By Sea
Cruise ships are now the main passenger liners from overseas which call at Melbourne, and they are not very frequent—in contrast to the 1950s and 1960s, when practically everyone travelled overseas by ship. The majority of ships are now container cargo vessels. There is only one regular sailing from Station Pier, Port Melbourne, two-and-a-half miles (4km) from the city centre: the *Abel Tasman*, which takes passengers on an overnight crossing to Tasmania three times a week.

Camping
There are many caravan parks near Melbourne and throughout Victoria, with a wide range of different accommodation available. You can take your own caravan or tent or stay in one of the on-site vans, cabins or self-contained units. They have varying amenities, including tennis courts, swimming pools and laundromats. There is a choice of settings—near the beach, near shops, or rural.

Badger Creek Caravan and Holiday Park, Don Road, Healesville (tel: (059) 62 4328), 38 miles (61km) from Melbourne. Set in a rural, bush area, with van and tent sites, units and cabins. Goats, donkeys, ducks and possums live there, too, and there are picnic areas with barbecues along the banks of Badger Creek.

Frankston Caravan Tourist Park, corner of Flinders and Robinson Roads, Frankston (tel: (059) 71 2333), 26 miles (42km) from Melbourne. It is near the beaches of the Mornington

provide scheduled services from capital cities to many places not served by the major airlines. Kendell Airlines are the main operators for Victoria.
Domestic Airlines operating within Victoria include:
Ansett Airlines, 465 Swanston Street (tel: 668 2222)
Australian Airlines, 50 Franklin Street (tel: 665 3333)
East West Airlines, second floor 230 Collins Street (tel: 653 3911)
Kendell Airlines, 431 Little Collins Street (tel: 670 2677 or 668 2222)

Peninsula. Van units with television, tennis court, swimming pool.

Melbourne Caravan Park, 265 Elizabeth Street, East Coburg (tel: 354 3533) is only six miles (10km) north of the city. It has on-site vans, self-contained units, a tent area and public transport from the park shop.

One of the newest parks is **Wantirna Park**, 203 Mountain Highway, Wantirna (tel: 887 1157), 15 miles (25km) from Melbourne. There are more than 200 grass sites, all fully serviced with water, electricity, natural gas, sewage facilities and barbecues. Modern cabins; four modern laundromats; swimming and wading pool; heated spa; tennis court.

A free directory of parks around Victoria can be obtained from the **Caravan Parks Association of Victoria** (tel: 569 9006) or from **Victour**, 230 Collins Street.

Chemist see **Pharmacies**

Crime
Melbourne is a safe city to visit. As in other large cities, there is a certain degree of crime, but usually common sense is the greatest safeguard.

Do not walk through the parks at night, particularly if you are alone. Even during the day it is wise to keep your eyes open. Wallets should not be in hip pockets, handbags not too loosely held—even when you are seated at a tram stop. There has been the odd occasion when

Mounted police show their horsepower on patrol in Banana Alley

the door of a passing car has opened and a pair of very quick hands has grabbed the handbag as the car sped off! For police and emergency numbers, see **Emergency Telephone Numbers**, page 114.

Customs Regulations

Visitors over 18 years of age are allowed to bring in the following goods duty free: one litre of alcoholic liquor, 200 cigarettes or 250 grams of cigars or tobacco and other dutiable goods up to the value of $400 for adults. Because Australia is free from many human, animal and plant diseases, the quarantine laws are strict. Foods, including salami and cheese and products made from plants, such as straw items; animals and items derived from protected wildlife, including furs, skin and ivory, are either prohibited or must undergo a quarantine examination.
If you are arriving in Victoria by car, train or coach, you are not permitted to bring fruit or seeds in from another state.
Penalties for drug offences are severe, and there are strict laws on the import of weapons and firearms.

Disabled Facilities

There is a mobility map giving access and facilities for people of limited mobility in central Melbourne. The booklet *A Day in the Open* gives similar information for national parks. Further information on all types of disability services in Victoria is available from the **Disabled Information Bureau Community Services Victoria**, sixth floor,

55 Swanston Street, City (tel: 653 6432).

Driving

A current driver's licence or an international driver's licence is necessary if you want to drive a car during your stay in Australia, and must be carried at all times when driving. International road signs are used, but in the countryside there may be some uniquely Australian signs, which are easily understood. The picture of a kangaroo or koala on a sign, for instance, means that kangaroos and koalas may cross the road.
Traffic keeps to the left side of the road. Drivers must give way to the right at unmarked sections. The speed limit in built up areas is 37mph (60kmph). Outside the built-up area, the maximum limit is 62.5mph (100kmph), unless otherwise indicated.
There are special rules for motorists regarding trams. A motorist must stop when a tram stops. You cannot pass a stationary tram unless told to do so by a uniformed tramway employee or a policeman. When you pass, the speed limit must not exceed 6mph (10kmph). At intersections, you must not move in front of or across a tram. Trams should always be passed on the left.
In the centre of Melbourne, at some intersections, you have to make a right hand turn from the left hand lane. Move left and wait for the traffic light to turn green before proceeding to turn right. The intersections where you do this are marked by signs overhead on wires, on the far

DIRECTORY

side of the intersection.
Melbourne is regarded as quite
an easy city for drivers.
Melbourne drivers, however, do
not have the best reputation.
Visiting drivers often find them
rude and impatient and not at all
willing to let them in on a traffic
line. Driving out of the city is
made easy, too, as many roads
are straight and long. The
journey to the Dandenongs is
practically a straight run, suburb
after suburb, for almost an hour
until you come to the foot of the
hills.
Seat belts must be worn by
drivers and all passengers, both
in the front and back seats. This
includes children. Young
children often need temporary
seats put into the car so they can
be 'belted up'. Passengers in
taxis must also wear seat belts.
There is a strict campaign
against drivers who drive under
the influence of alcohol. Police
can stop drivers for random
breathalyser tests. Many people
now going to a hotel to drink or
to a restaurant or party, tend to
leave their cars at home and
take a taxi. The safest advice is
not to drink at all if you intend to
drive.
Fuel: There are many fuel
stations easily identifiable
around Melbourne and
throughout Victoria, selling
leaded or unleaded fuel. Prices
can differ slightly at different
stations; in the country, fuel is a
little more expensive.

Motoring Clubs
Members of the Automobile
Association (AA) of Britain, or
associations affiliated to the
Commonwealth Motoring

Conference (CMC), can make
use of the reciprocal
arrangements with motoring
clubs in Australia.
Each state has its own
association, which can provide
you with maps and other
publications, the highway code,
and breakdown assistance.
Remember to bring your
membership card to qualify for
help.
The **Royal Automobile Club of
Victoria (RACV)**, is based at 123
Queen Street, City (tel: 607 2233).

The RACV has a Travel Centre at 136 Exhibition Street (tel: 650 3983).

Driving is an ideal way to see natural attractions – especially the more remote areas

Car Rental

To hire a car you need a current Australian, overseas or international driver's licence. Most car rental companies also ask for a major international credit card or a cash deposit of at least $40. Minimum age is either 21 or 25; this varies from one company to another. Rental costs also vary, but unlimited free kilometres in metropolitan areas are usually included in the rates. Companies include **Hertz** (tel: 663 6244). **Avis** (tel: 663 6366). **Budget** (tel: 320 6333). **Rent A Bomb Car** (tel: 429 4003) is a cheap option; the cars are older and are for use only in the metropolitan area.

Refer to the Yellow Pages under the entry of Motor Car Rentals to obtain details of other rental firms.

There are many fly/drive packages available with holidays to Australia, offering discount car rental and accommodation; your travel agent will advise you.

Electricity
The electric current throughout Australia is 240 volts AC 50HZ, with a three-pin power outlet. Adaptors may be needed for electric appliances brought from overseas, plus a voltage converter for appliances without a dual-voltage facility which normally run on a lower voltage. Most hotels and motels have 110 volt outlets for shavers.

Embassies and Consulates
Embassies are located in Canberra; most countries are represented in Melbourne by Consulate Generals.

American Consulate General
24 Albert Road, South Melbourne (tel: 697 7900; after hours: 648 1583; visitor visa information: 699 2425).

British Consulate General
330 Collins Street, Melbourne (tel: 670 5169).

Canadian Consulate General
1 Collins Street, Melbourne (tel: 54 1433).

New Zealand Consulate General
330 Collins Street, Melbourne (tel: 670 8111).

Consulates for other countries are listed in the telephone book, in the white pages.

Emergency Telephone Numbers
For emergency calls to ambulance, fire brigade and police, dial 000. No charge is made for the call.

Other emergencies:

Ambulance 11440
Fire Brigade 11441
Police 11444

Life Line (personal emergencies) 662 1000

Personal Emergency Service 529 4000
Poisons Information Centre 345 5678
Dental Emergency Service 341 0222

Accident Towing Service 546 4000

Doctors are listed in the Yellow Pages under 'Medical Practitioners'. Some are listed under suburbs.

Entertainment Information
Three daily newspapers— *The Melbourne Age, Sun News Pictorial* and *The Herald*—give great coverage of the entertainment scene, with daily lists of programmes for cinemas. On Friday, *The Melbourne Age* has a pull-out supplement entertainment guide, which gives details of just about everything that is on in Melbourne.
The Herald also has an entertainment guide, called After Hours, published on Thursday.
Sun News Pictorial has an entertainment listings in its Friday edition.
Beat, a free weekly newspaper,

gives full coverage to the young contemporary scene in the greatest detail.

Other free weekly guides include *This Week in Melbourne* and *Discover Melbourne*, available at **Victour**, 230 Collins Street, and in hotels.

An information line, *What's On in Melbourne*, can be obtained by dialling 0055 34360.

Health Regulations

You are not required to have any vaccinations or inoculations for entry into Australia. The exception is if you have left, within six days, a country infected with yellow fever and recognised as such by Australia, in which case you will need a valid yellow fever vaccination certificate.

Tap water is safe to drink.

If you do become ill and need to consult a doctor, there are medical centres which you can attend without appointment. If you hold a British passport you have the benefit of access to Australia's healthcare system, Medicare. This entitles you to treatment as a public patient in a public hospital and treatment by doctors in private practice. There is a charge, and these services are only for visitors who become ill while in Australia and require treatment before returning home. For further information, contact **Medicare**, GPO Box 9822, in all capital cities. Visitors who think they may need medical treatment should take out a travel insurance policy which includes medical treatment during absence from home.

Medications: visitors are permitted to bring in reasonable quantities of prescribed (non-narcotic) medications, which should be labelled. For large quantities, you should have a doctor's certificate to produce to Customs if necessary. Local pharmacists can make up most overseas prescriptions but they must be written by a Victorian-registered doctor.

Holidays

Australia has many national holidays, and states have additional holidays of their own. School holidays differ in each state.

Public Holidays

1 January: New Year's Day

26 January: Australia Day (on this date or the following Monday)

March, second Monday: Labour Day

March/April: Easter (Good Friday, Easter Monday). Easter Tuesday is a bank holiday.

25 April: Anzac Day

June, second Monday: Queen's Birthday

September, last Tuesday: Show Day (Melbourne only)

November, first Tuesday: Melbourne Cup (Melbourne only)

25 December: Christmas Day

26 December: Boxing Day

School Holidays

Tourist resorts are more crowded during school holidays, which are taken four times a year in Melbourne and Victoria. The main summer holiday is approximately five-and-a-half weeks from late December; then there are two-and-a-half weeks in April, July and September–October.

DIRECTORY

Media

Newspapers

There are two morning newspapers in Melbourne: *The Melbourne Age*, a broadsheet, and *The Sun News Pictorial*, a popular tabloid. They are published daily from Monday to Saturday. *The Melbourne Age* has special sections and pull-out supplements during the week, with excellent directory guides and detailed information on a wide range of subjects. On Tuesday there is Epicure for wining and dining, and on Friday the Entertainment Guide, printed on yellow paper. Saturday's edition has a special section on the Arts.

The Herald, which celebrated its 150th year in 1990, is the only afternoon newspaper. It gives a very wide coverage of all that is happening in Melbourne as well

Football can always make headlines

as the main overseas news. It also has special sections: the Taste guide to food and wine on Wednesday, and, on Thursday, After Hours, for entertainment. On Saturday the Arts are covered.

The Australian is a national newspaper, specially strong on world news. It has a colour magazine on Saturday.

The *Australian Financial Review* is the business newspaper, published from Monday to Friday.

On Sundays there are three newspapers: *The Sunday Age*, the *Sunday Herald* and *The Sunday Sun*.

There is also a range of local ethnic newspapers in foreign languages.

Magazines

As well as glossy magazines from the US and Europe, local magazines cover all interests. Australia has its own edition of *Vogue* and *Vogue Living*, and the top women's weekly magazine is *New Idea*. The *Australian Women's Weekly*, for so long an Australian weekly institution, is now published monthly.

The top business magazine is *Business Review Weekly*, known as *BRW*. *The Bulletin* is a weekly magazine covering all news, and incorporates *Newsweek*. Newspapers and magazines are available at newsagents. There are street stands in the city when editions come out in the morning and afternoon. Some ethnic newspapers are sold in newsagents, but are more readily available at appropriate ethnic stores.

Some overseas newspapers such as the *London Times* and *New York Times* are sold in Melbourne. They are usually a few days later than the date of publication. The best place for these and interstate Australian newspapers is at **McGills Authorized Newsagency**, 187 Elizabeth Street, City (tel: 602 5566).

Radio
There are more than 20 radio stations on the AM and FM bands. The **Australian Broadcasting Corporation**, ABC, has three stations. **3AR Radio National**, has emphasis on music and the arts; **3LO** on news and current affairs, and **ABC FM** concentrates on classical music. Ethnic stations are **3EA** on AM and **ZZZ** on FM. The broadcasts are in several foreign languages including Aboriginal.
Radio Australia, Australia's international station, has an audience of about 50 million. It is a shortwave station, broadcasting in English, Indonesian, Standard Chinese, Cantonese, Tok Pisin (for Papua New Guinea), French, Thai, Japanese and Vietnamese. Within Australia, the English service can be heard from midnight to 05.30 hrs Monday and 01.00–05.30 hrs Tuesday to Sunday on the ABC Radio National Network (3AR). Free guides to Radio Australia's programmes and frequencies are published regularly. Copies are available if you phone 235 2360 (open line recorded message) or write to Radio Australia Programme Guide, GPO Box 428G, Melbourne,

Victoria 3001.

Television
There are five television stations, including three commercial channels: Channels 7, 9 and 10. The two non-commercial channels are Channel 2, which is part of the Australian Broadcasting Corporation, the multi-cultural SBS—28UHF, which has a great reputation for its international news and sports coverage.
The Melbourne Age publishes a Green Guide on Thursdays with detailed daily programme guides for radio and television for the forthcoming week.

Money Matters

Currency
Australia uses the decimal currency system: 100 cents to one dollar. Denominations for coins are one, two, five, 10, 20 and 50 cents (), $1 and $2; and for notes, $5, $10, $20, $50 and $100. Each note is a different colour and the size increases with its value.

Money Exchange
There is no restriction on the personal funds you can bring into Australia, but you cannot take out more than five thousand dollars in Australian currency without approval from the **Reserve Bank of Australia**, 60 Collins Street, City (tel: 653 8555). There is no limit on travellers' cheques in Australian dollars, or currency notes for other countries.
Foreign currency notes and travellers' cheques can be exchanged for Australian currency at banks and major

DIRECTORY

hotels.

It is advisable to have travellers' cheques in Australian dollars for use in Australia.

Credit Cards

Major credit cards are widely accepted in shops, restaurants, taxis. The main cards recognised are American Express, Diners Club, Visa and Mastercard.

Bankcard is an Australian credit card.

Lost credit cards should be reported at the appropriate offices:

American Express: tel: (008) 230 100 (local call fee only)

Diners Club: tel: 320 8888

Visa: tel: (008) 224 402

Barclay Visa: tel: (008) 224 548

Mastercard: tel: 665 2755 (after hours (008) 224 402)

Departure Tax

Before leaving Australia, every person over 12 years of age must pay a $10 departure tax. Tax stamps can be purchased at the airport or any post office and must be paid for in Australian currency.

Opening Times

Once upon a time opening times for most establishments were precise and clear-cut. Now they are changing and extending. It was once said that Melbourne closed on Sundays and this is still true of the centre of the city, though some small shops within hotel complexes and Chinatown, and shopping complexes and food shops in the suburbs are open. Saturday afternoon retail trading has only been introduced in recent years. General opening hours are given below, but there are often exceptions, so it is advisable to check.

Banks

Open in city and suburbs:
Monday to Thursday
09.30–16.30 hrs; Friday
09.30–17.00 hrs.
Some city banks open from
08.00–18.00 hrs.
Closed on Saturday, Sunday and public holidays and Easter Tuesday. The Bank of Melbourne opens on Saturday
09.00–12.00 hrs.

Business Offices

Office hours are generally from Monday to Friday
09.00–17.30 hrs. All offices are closed Saturday, Sunday and public holidays.

Department Stores and Shops

City and suburban shops generally open Monday to Thursday 09.00–17.30 hrs; Friday 09.00–21.00 hrs; and Saturday 09.00–17.00 hrs.

Small provision shops, often called milk bars or delicatessens, usually open seven days a week.

Supermarkets generally have longer hours, and some shops and supermarkets are open in Victoria Street, Abbotsford (the Vietnamese area), on Sundays. The South Melbourne market is open on Sunday.

Licensing hours for public bars are generally 10.00–22.00 hrs. Sunday hours vary.

Newsagents

Monday to Friday
07.00–18.00 hrs; Saturday
07.00–13.00 hrs; Sunday
07.00–13.00 hrs.

Post Offices

General Post Office (GPO) at the corner of Bourke and Elizabeth Streets opens Monday to Friday 08.00–18.00 hrs; Saturday 08.00–12.00 hrs. Stamp vending machine operates 24 hours a day. Suburban post offices Monday to Friday 09.00–17.00 hrs.

Personal Safety

Deadly snakes, spiders and sharks do exist in Australia, but most Australians have never encountered any—especially in the cities. However, precautions can be taken.

Sharks

Sharks can be sighted near bayside or ocean beaches, but they are rare in the bay. During the summer lifesavers on the beaches keep a lookout for sharks and there are planes patrolling above the bayside and ocean beaches with professional shark spotters. If an alarm bell is sounded, leave the water as quickly as possible.

Swimming in Melbourne and Victoria is generally very safe, but always swim between the flags if they are on the beaches. If you do get into any difficulty swimming, raise your hand. Swimmers everywhere are advised not to go straight in the water after a substantial meal, and *never* dive into water without knowing its depth.

Snakes

There are anti-venoms for all the main groups of dangerous species of snakes in Australia. The most common snakes in Victoria are the tiger snake, brown snake, copper head and red-bellied black snake, but snakes are rarely found in Melbourne except in outer suburbs.

To avoid being bitten, when in the bush, look where you are walking. Wear stout shoes and never put your hands into hollow logs or long grass without looking. Use a torch in the bush at night. If you do see a snake, leave it alone.

If you are bitten, keep calm and move as little as possible. Very little venom reaches the bloodstream if firm pressure is applied over the bitten area and the limb is immobilised. Do not remove any clothing, as this could help the poison circulate. Keep the limb as still as possible; if possible, bandage the limb and bind some type of splint to it. Do not cut or wash the bitten area, and do not suck out the venom; the snake may be identified by the venom on the skin.

Spiders

The red back spider is the most dangerous spider that you could come in contact with in Melbourne or Victoria. It is easily identifiable by the brilliant red stripe on its black back. You are unlikely to be bitten by a spider, but if you are, don't panic: pain from a bite is severe, but the venom acts very slowly, and the anti-venom is widely available and effective.

Insects

European wasps have become a pest in recent years. They can fly into cans or bottles or glasses, so look before you drink!

Flies are not harmful, but very annoying. They are inclined to stick to you unless you wave

DIRECTORY

them away—an action that has become known as the Great Australian Wave!

Mosquitoes can leave an itchy mark, but there is no other harm done. You can use insect repellant to keep them away, or special burning coils if you are sitting outside.

Sunburn

The sun can be the greatest hazard to visitors, specially those with fair skins. Wear a protective sun-screen, particularly on the face. Advice on the most appropriate strength for your type of skin can be sought at pharmacies or stores. The sun-screens should be applied half an hour before going out into the sun and re-applied every couple of hours.

On the beach, wear a hat or sit under an umbrella.

Pharmacies

Overseas prescriptions must be written by a Victorian-registered doctor. Pharmacies sell brands of general medication which are familiar the world over, and some open for long hours.

City

O'Neale's Pharmacy, 206 Bourke Street, Village Cinema Centre, (tel: 663 3339); open seven days a week 09.00–21.00 hrs.

Prahran

Leonard Long Pharmacy, corner of William and High Streets, Prahran (tel: 51 3977 or 51 6130); open every day of the year 08.00–24.00 hrs.

Toorak

C Wallis & Son, 426 Toorak Road, Toorak (tel: 240 1211); open every day of the year 09.00–21.00 hrs.

For other pharmacies, see the Yellow Pages under 'Chemists–Pharmaceutical'.

Places of Worship

There are places of worship for all major religions in the city of Melbourne and its suburbs, and in country towns in Victoria. Some of the major places are:

Anglican

St James' Old Cathedral, corner of King and Batman Streets, West Melbourne (tel: 329 6133).
St Paul's Cathedral, corner of Flinders and Swanston Streets (tel: 650 3791).
St Peter's Eastern Hill, 469 Albert Street, City (tel: 662 2391).

Baptist

Collins Street Baptist Church, 174 Collins Street (tel: 650 1180).

Jewish

Melbourne Hebrew Congregation, corner of Arnold Street and Toorak Road, South Yarra (tel: 266 2255).

Presbyterian

Scots Church, corner of Russell and Collins Street (tel: 650 9903 or 650 9904).

Roman Catholic

St Francis' Church, 312 Lonsdale Street (tel: 663 2495).
St Patrick's Cathedral, Albert Street, East Melbourne (tel: 662 2233).

Uniting Church (a unity of Presbyterian, Methodist and Congregational Churches), 110 Collins Street (tel: 654 5120 or 654 8685).

Police

Members of the Victorian Police Force are distinguished by their

Waiting for news in the bush

navy blue uniforms and pale blue shirts, and hats with checked bands.

Parking police, who check motor vehicles against infringements and overstaying on parking meters, wear a paler shade of blue.

Police often direct traffic at busy intersections, and there are police on horseback, mainly in attendance for ceremonies or where there are crowds assembled for a special event. There are many patrol cars, clearly marked, driving around the streets in city and suburbs.

Post Office

The main post office in Melbourne is the General Post Office (GPO), situated at the corner of Bourke and Elizabeth Street (tel: 609 4265). There are post offices, too in most shopping centres (see **Opening Times** for business hours). An after-hours courier service, **Express Courier Base**, is in Stanley Street, West Melbourne. Letter boxes are painted red.

If you would like mail held for you at the GPO, have it addressed to:

c/o Poste Restante, GPO, Melbourne, Victoria 3001

In the Galleria Shopping Plaza, ground level, at the corner of Bourke and Elizabeth Streets (opposite the GPO), a Post Shop sells stamps, philatelic products and packaging, and Australiana. (open: Monday to Thursday 09.00–17.30 hrs; Friday 09.00–21.00 hrs; Saturday 09.00–13.00 hrs).

Public Transport

The public transport system of Melbourne is known as The Met.

DIRECTORY

Trams are still a favourite way of getting around the city

Trains and trams form the basis of the system, which covers the metropolitan area, with buses providing additional services. It is one of the best urban systems in Australia, and one ticket can be used for all three.

Trains
Electric trains, starting from Flinders Street Station, serve the major suburban areas, while interstate and country trains leave from Spencer Street Station.
Melbourne's Underground Rail Loop connects all lines. There are stations at Flagstaff Museum, Parliament, Flinders and Spencer Streets.

Trams
Distinctive green and gold coloured electric trams operate in a 12.5 mile (20km) radius of the city. The main services run from Swanston and Elizabeth Streets (north/south); Flinders, Collins and Bourke Streets and Batman Avenue (east/west).

Buses
These operate from the central business district to Middle Brighton, La Trobe University, Deer Park West, Woori Yalloc and North Altona.

The Met is divided into three zones. There is a series of flat rate fares, depending on which zone(s) you travel in, and for how long. There are three-hour and one-day tickets offering unlimited travel; for longer stays in Melbourne it may be worth your while purchasing a weekly or monthly pass.

The system is explained by excellent free booklets obtainable from any rail station, bus or tram depot, or from the Met office at 103 Elizabeth Street. Further information is available from the **Met Transport Information Centre** (tel: 617 0900). A map of the system is available from the Victour office, 230 Collins Street, and at bookshops and newsstands. The Met's normal hours of operation are from 05.00 to midnight, Monday to Friday, with reduced services at weekends and holidays.

Country and Interstate Services

V/Line operate rail and coach services out of Melbourne to country Victoria and to other states. Services depart from the country and interstate terminal—Spencer Street Station (tel: 619 5000). Bookings may be made here or in person at major stations.

For information on sightseeing coach tours in or around Melbourne and Victoria see **Tour Companies**, page 124.

Taxis

Taxis may be hailed on the street, at taxi ranks, at major hotels or called by phone. Fares depend on the time of day and distance. There are three tariff bandings:

Tariff One—06.00–18.00 hrs Monday to Friday;
Tariff Two—between 20.00 hrs and midnight, weekends and

public holidays;
Tariff Three—midnight to 06.00 hrs every day.
In addition there is a flag fall charge and a service booking fee.

Companies:
Arrow (tel: 417 1111); **Astoria** (tel: 347 5511); **Regal Combined** (tel: 810 0222); **Silver Top** (tel: 345 2455).
Others appear in the Yellow Pages.

Student and Youth Travel

Overseas students under 26 years *may* get a discount on normal economy fares to Australia, but not automatically. Identification is needed in the form of an International Student Identity Card or an international airline ticket issued at a student discount.

For Youth Hostels see **Accommodation**, page 86.
Out of term-time, the University of Melbourne offers its halls of residence to travellers; lower rates are given to students.

Telephones

Public telephones are quite easy to find around the city and suburbs. Some are at suburban post offices, some in glass booths in the streets; and there are telephones available in some hotel foyers and department stores. They usually take 10, 20 or 50 cents and $1 coins. Charges are set, with no time limit for local calls. Numbers starting with 008 are interstate, but a local fee is charged. Subscriber Trunk Dialling (STD) calls outside the Melbourne zone are charged on the distance and the time. Calls are cheaper from 22.00 to 08.00 hrs, Monday to

Friday, and from 18.00 on Saturday to 08.00 hrs on Monday. International Direct Dial (IDD) is possible at **Payphones**, Telecom Australia, 175 Elizabeth Street (open 24 hours).

To call Melbourne from overseas, dial the international access code, then the Australia country code 61, followed by 3 (the Melbourne area code minus the initial '0'), and finally the subscribers' number.

To call overseas from Australia, dial the international access code 0011, then the country code (44 for the United Kingdom; 353 for the Republic of Ireland; 1 for the US and Canada; and 64 for New Zealand), followed by the city code minus the initial '0', and finally the subscriber's number.

Time
Victoria is on Eastern Standard time, 10 hours ahead of Greenwich Mean Time. It changes by an hour during summer, when Daylight Saving is introduced. From the end of October to early March, clocks are put forward one hour.

The Eastern States of Australia, Victoria, New South Wales and Queensland, are all on Eastern Standard Time. South Australia is half an hour behind, Western Australia two hours behind. New Zealand is two hours ahead. New York and Toronto are 15 hours behind, and San Francisco and Vancouver are 18 hours behind for most of the year.

Tipping
Australians, traditionally, do not tip very much, except perhaps in top restaurants where 10 to 15 per cent would be added to the bill depending on service.

Service charges are not normally added to hotel and restaurant bills. Railway porters have set charges; hotel porters you may tip for service. Others, including, for instance, hairdressers and airport porters, do not expect to be tipped.

Toilets
There are public toilets for women in the city's three department stores. In David Jones' rest rooms there is a separate room for mothers who wish to attend to their babies. In Myer, there is a larger rest room with a television set.

Cast-iron urinals are situated in various parts of the city.

There are many public toilets for men and women in the city; the most central is outside the GPO in Elizabeth Street, and others are based opposite the Queen Victoria Market and beside the Town Hall in Collins Street.

Tour Companies
Coach companies which run daily sightseeing tours in Melbourne and the main Victorian attractions include:
Ansett Pioneer Tours, 465 Swanston Street (tel: 668 2422) Their trips include the Dandenongs, the fairy penguins at Phillip Island, Ballarat and the Great Ocean Road.

Australian Pacific Tours, 181 Flinders Street (tel: 650 1511)

A **City Explorer** double-decker bus (tel: 619 9444) makes a circular tour of the city, calling at attractions such as the Zoo, Lygon Street, Carlton and Old Melbourne Gaol. You can stop and rejoin the bus on the same ticket. It operates daily from Flinders Street Station, every

hour 09.00–16.00 hrs.

Express Coaches travel to interstate capital cities and other major towns and are the cheapest means of travel. Coach companies include **Ansett Pioneer** (tel: 668 2422) and **Greyhound** (tel: 668 2666). You can book seats through the **Interstate Bus Service** (tel: 654 8477).

V/line (tel: 619 5000) has combined train and coach tours to the wine town of Rutherglen, Echuca and Queenscliff.

Melbourne Heritage Walks with Maxine Wood (tel: 241 1985) take approximately one and a half hours on weekdays or weekends and accept a maximum of 10 people.

The Great Ocean Road lives up to its name, with spectacular sea views

Tourist Offices
Victorian Tourism Commission offices overseas:

Canada
second floor, 113 Davenport Road, Toronto, Ontario M5RH8 (tel: (416) 960 3533).

New Zealand
15th Floor, Quay Tower, 29 Customs Street West, Auckland (tel: (9) 79 4566).

UK
Office of the Agent-General, Victoria House, Melbourne Place, The Strand, London WC2B 4LG (tel: (071) 836 2656).

USA

2121 Avenue of the Stars, Suite 1270, Los Angeles, California 90067 (tel: (213) 553 6352).

LANGUAGE

Australians speak English—with an accent, which has been described as nasal and lazy. An oft-given example to illustrate the accent is that 'day' can sound like 'die'. The Australian vernacular is referred to as 'Strine'—which is what the word 'Australian' is reputed to sound like in a strong Aussie accent. However, you will find that not every Australian speaks Strine!

There is, in fact, a multicultural influence on the Australia of today. You may hear Greek, Italian, Cantonese, Japanese, Turkish or Vietnamese spoken on the street. Aboriginal languages have left their mark on Australian place-names, but their influence is not very evident in Victoria.

Here is a list of some words which are commonly used in Australia:

Magical Melbourne: a star of a city, by day or by night

arvo afternoon
barbie barbecue
beaut beautiful, very good
bush natural country
chook chicken
crook ill, bad, angry—to go 'crook' at
daks trousers
dill stupid
footy football
grog alcoholic drink
ocker loud-mouthed Australian
outback isolated country (not in Victoria)
Oz Australia
plonk cheap wine
knocks criticises
no worries don't mention it—in reply to thanks
sheila young woman
she'll be right, mate everything will be okay
shoot through leave, depart
schooner tall glass of beer, a measure of beer. Beer can be ordered by the schooner
shout buy—a round of drinks
snags sausages
stubby small bottle of beer
tube, tinny can of beer
tucker food
uni university
ute utility truck (with an open back)
wheels a car
wowser killjoy

INDEX

INDEX/ACKNOWLEDGEMENTS

The Automobile Association would like to thank the following photographers and libraries for their assistance in the preparation of this book:

CHRISTINE OSBORNE (CHRISTINE OSBORNE PICTURES) took all the photographs (© AA Photo Library) in this book, except:

MELBOURNE TOURIST BOARD Cover, 92 Cricketers Bar, 94 *Puffing Billy*, 104 Skiing, 106 Tennis, 88 Concert Hall organ, 89 Princess Theatre.

NATURE PHOTOGRAPHERS LTD 52 Black swan (P R Sterry) 57 Budgies (W Giersberger) 58 Red kangaroo (S C Bisserot) 59 Crimson rosella (K Carlson) 60 Scarlet robin (R S Daniel) 62 Greenhood orchid (B Burbidge)

SPECTRUM COLOUR LIBRARY 14 Flinders Street Station, 24 Como House, 33 Victorian Arts Centre, 35 Royal Exhibition Building, 38 Shrine of Remembrance, 40 Collins Street, 74 Queen Victoria monument, 93 *Polly Woodside*, 95 Beach, 96/7 Moomba festival.

ZEFA PICTURE LIBRARY UK LTD 17 Skyscrapers, 87 Skyline by night, 108 Port of Melbourne.